Flying Start

FLYING START:
Mentoring for Air Force Company Grade Officers

By Colonel John C. Liburdi, USAF (Ret.)

This book is dedicated to Air Force Tactical Air Control Party members, of all ranks, who courageously direct Close Air Support strikes in the most hostile areas of the battlespace.

Copyright Data:

Copyright © 2009 by John C. Liburdi

All rights reserved. No part of this book may be reproduced, stored, or transmitted by any means—whether auditory, graphic, mechanical, or electronic—without written permission of both publisher and author, except in the case of brief excerpts used in critical articles and reviews. Unauthorized reproduction of any part of this work is illegal and is punishable by law.

ISBN: 978-0-557-06065-8

This book has not been indorsed, approved or authorized by the U.S. Air Force or any other element of the Department of Defense.

Contents

INTRODUCTION 1

Chapter 1 WARRIOR PREPARATION 5

Chapter 2 PROFESSIONAL KNOWLEDGE 15

Chapter 3 PURPOSEFUL PRESENCE 23

Chapter 4 IMAGE PROJECTION 29

Chapter 5 DYNAMIC LEADERSHIP 39

Chapter 6 PRACTICAL MANAGEMENT 55

Chapter 7 EFFECTIVE COMMUNICATIONS 67

Chapter 8 BULLETPROOF CONDUCT 77

Chapter 9 BOSS RELATIONS 89

Chapter 10 CAREER PROGRESSION 99

Chapter 11 PARTING THOUGHTS 109

ABOUT THE AUTHOR 111

INTRODUCTION

Let me join the many who are welcoming you to the Air Force officer corps. By now you surely realize that you haven't merely found an occupation; rather, you've answered a noble calling—the profession of arms. You'll soon discover that the Air Force is an incredibly wholesome institution that has teamwork as its premise and the protection of our nation as its mission. As a young officer, your role in the Air Force may initially seem rather small, but the magnitude and scope of that role will start to grow exponentially as you successfully meet a series of exciting challenges.

The Air Force guides and nurtures its young officers to become tomorrow's great leaders. Generally speaking, mistakes made early on in one's career quickly fade from view as success prevails. However, too many mistakes or the wrong type of mistake could jeopardize the mission or lead to career flameout. Obviously, your career as an officer is bound to rise far above mere survival. And, you certainly want to avoid any and all of the classic "What was I thinking?" scenarios. To help ensure that happens, my book provides a host of lessons learned and valuable insights that can help you succeed in the Air Force environment.

The structure of this book is essentially a toolbox, loaded with tactics, techniques and procedures that allow you to profit from the experiences of those who came before you. The mentoring in the following ten chapters is a collection of informative "data bursts," each one addressing a separate aspect of officership. The straight talk you'll see is simply an effort to share some valuable information; no one is being so presumptuous as to talk down to you. In order to avoid awkward wording, I routinely refer to officers as "he," but readers should feel free to mentally interchange the pronouns he and she throughout this book.

It will quickly become apparent that the content of this book consciously flies in the face of the old adage, "Some things are better left unsaid." But that's acceptable because the act of reading the book is essentially an academic exercise; thus, nobody gets hurt. You may feel that some of my advice is not particularly relevant to your individual circumstances, especially if you're currently in the cockpit or deployed downrange. Be that as it may, you can rest assured that most of the issues covered here will eventually pop up on the radar screen during your career. Forewarned is forearmed; the insight you gain here will have you better prepared to determine the way ahead as these various types of situations unfold.

Most of the lessons-learned contained herein reflect positive events that occurred during my unusually long forty-year active duty career; obviously, I'm reluctant to divulge whether or not I had to personally learn any of these lessons the hard way. However, I will say that the hypothetical aspects of this book are not founded entirely on fiction. Nothing was held back in the effort to help young officers get their Air Force careers off to a flying start, no matter whether it's a four-year stint or a full thirty-year career. As you begin to progress in your career, always bear in mind that a military officer's success is not measured solely in terms of rank; actually, it's defined more by the level of excellence and honor the officer achieves in the eyes of his comrades-in-arms.

Colonel John C. Liburdi
USAF (Ret.)

Chapter 1
WARRIOR PREPARATION

In this era of highly advanced technology, airmen can remotely strike overseas targets from facilities on U.S. bases or conduct overseas strike missions by flying roundtrip from U.S. bases. But in most instances, the airmen rotate to foreign countries for relatively short tours of duty in a hostile fire zone. So it's necessary for all officers to stay tempered in a physical sense, to stay prepared in a logistical sense, and to get mentally postured for successful deployments. Here are a few things to contemplate in anticipation of your first overseas deployment.

Get smart on the overseas Area of Responsibility prior to your deployment. This includes the geography, culture, religion, political picture, location of friendly forces, and the overall status of the military operation. Two good starting points are the *World Factbook* located on the CIA's website (www.cia.gov) and *Country Studies* found on the State Department's website (www.state.gov). Other information that's of a classified nature can be searched out by accessing the appropriate major command and combatant command websites on the secure version of the internet, referred to as the "SIPRNet."

Learn what mission systems and equipment are being used at the location you're deploying to. Before deploying, familiarize yourself with the overall concept of employment for those systems. Visit local facilities in your area that have the same type systems, and talk to the people who operate and maintain them. You may also be able to dialogue with fellow airmen who recently returned from the base you're deploying to. Take some time to search out Air Force and joint lessons-learned documents on military websites so that you can learn about and avoid any related pitfalls that your fellow airmen have experienced in the past.

Become generally familiar with the basic principles of Air Operations. This includes procedures for planning and executing Air Operations and the various sensor-to-shooter systems used to find, fix and destroy targets. Instead of engaging in a mundane academic exercise, get all this into focus by touring a Combined Air Operations Center. Take time to walk through all of the planning and execution cycle functions and to view all the systems that are utilized in the process. Rather than visit a dormant AOC, make your visit during an ongoing operation or exercise so that you can see all the elements actually in play.

Learn how to use the secure telephone, secure internet, secure fax, secure radio, and secure conferencing systems. You'll encounter much of the same equipment downrange. Stay focused whenever you're dealing with classified data and equipment. Consider the foreign officer who was transporting a secure laptop computer back to headquarters after a classified briefing. The briefing went so well that his promotion seemed imminent, thus prompting him to stop at a luxury car dealer to window shop. While doing so, the computer was stolen from his car. Fortunately, the thief discovered war planning documents on the computer and turned it over to the police. The thief was praised for his patriotism, but the officer's career went down in flames.

As an Air Force officer, you should be able to recognize and have a general knowledge of at least a few of the aircraft currently in the Air Force inventory, particularly those that operate in the theater to which you're deploying. This might include the roles and capabilities of some of the Air Force's primary airframes such as the B2 Spirit, C-130 Hercules, F-16 Falcon, F-35 Lightning II, V-22 Osprey, MQ-1 Predator, and so on. For your personal gratification, you might want to pick one of your absolute favorite vintage aircraft and get familiar with its capabilities and history. Among those venerable aircraft would be the P-38 Lightning and the B-36 Peacemaker.

Endeavor to become an expert small arms marksman, at least with the sidearm. Also take advantage of any opportunity to receive specialized handgun training for close quarters combat, a vital skill in an urban warfare setting. Those basic fighting skills need to be routinely honed, even if the immediate motive is only to satisfy personal pride. Although Air Force officers are focused on airpower, there are times when soldier skills are required to fight and win. You have to be able to contribute to victory in a hostile fire situation on the ground, particularly in Air Base Defense scenarios and in joint operations. Plus, firing various types of weapons on the range is a truly exhilarating experience.

Keep your other war skills training up to date. Some of the recurring classes are often rather perfunctory, so be sure to get a last dose of that training just before departing on your deployment. You'll readily absorb the procedures because you'll be closer to doing it for real. Have your special equipment issued to you as early as possible so you have ample time to check sizing and get familiar with it before deploying. Also, keep your immunizations current; it's difficult and ineffective to get all of your shots at one time, just moments before you board the aircraft headed for the overseas location you're deploying to.

The duty day in the deployed environment is likely to be far more physically demanding than at home station, and it will surely be a lot longer during hostilities. Plus, climate and terrain have to be factored into the anticipated setting. Therefore, develop and maintain the physical stamina that will allow you to go the distance, and even a little beyond, so that you can always lead the pack from the front. You'll also find yourself to be much more alert and perceptive when you're in shape; thus, you'll have heightened situational awareness.

While it hardly seems to be a war-fighting skill, there's great benefit in learning to speed read documents and e-mails. Likewise, it's smart to train yourself to quickly focus on just the key elements of briefing slides and video displays, particularly ones that are cluttered with too many details. Training yourself to rapidly and accurately digest data is not just a time management strategy, it can be a critical skill in battle management settings, such as command posts and air operations centers where there's continuous information overload. It's also essential to learn some of the jargon and acronyms commonly used by air campaign managers, such as TST, AR, TOT, Shack, BDA, etc.

Some officers might find aesthetics to be essential in their life; however, there'll be little opportunity to maintain that Hollywood image at a down-range location. There aren't any hair color kits or private bathrooms available in the tactical setting or at a forward operating base. Colored contact lenses are a similar consideration; you can't wear them while fine sand and strong wind is blowing into your eyes. In fact, officers who have vision issues ought to consider undergoing LASIK surgery by a military ophthalmologist so that they no longer need contact lenses, eyeglasses and gas mask inserts. Do bring along a couple pairs of high-tech sunglasses that wrap close to the face (no trademark logos allowed on the sunglasses).

Prior to deployment, get all of your personal affairs organized so that they'll pretty much run on autopilot. Set up bill payments via automatic deductions, preferably from a checking account rather than a credit card. That's because you would have to reestablish all of the automatic bill payments in the event you were the victim of credit card fraud. Most bases have secure parking lots for the cars of deployed personnel, and insurance companies will provide a premium rebate covering the period of deployment. If you own a house, arrange for regular lawn service and for the police to occasionally check on your home. You may need to create a current will and power of attorney, both done for free at the base legal office. If you're married, be sure to remind the commander and the first sergeant that your spouse is remaining in the local area.

Once you're well established at your first duty location, let your boss know that you're ready to go on any short deployment or down-range visit that may come up, the sooner the better. Your initial deployment will get you familiar with the transportation procedures and the tactical environment. That is, you'll know how to get down range and where you fit into the tactical setting. The first trip will also provide a good shakedown of your uniforms and gear. After your first immersion in the overseas tactical setting, you'll be pretty much primed to hit the deck running on subsequent deployments throughout your career.

Stay postured for deployments; live and travel light. Get new Airman Battle Uniforms issued and tailored early, with proper name tape, service tape, specialty badge, and rank insignia permanently sewn on. Check to be sure your dog tags are on hand; if not, get new ones punched. Buy a quality penlight and a pocketknife with tools. Obtain comfortable earplugs for those noisy tactical airlift flights. Don't go on deployments carrying fashionable or flimsy luggage that will self-destruct in transportation channels; you need luggage that's rugged and lockable. Add a web belt around each piece of luggage, and attach a bright baggage tag so that you can quickly find your gear when it's in the middle of a big pile at the tactical air terminal.

Never complain about living conditions or the harsh climate upon arrival at the deployed location. Griping wouldn't improve anything and it would probably demoralize others; just cowboy up! If you're leading a team down range, do everything within your power to ensure that your troops are properly settled in and that their basic needs are met before getting comfortable yourself. This is particularly true in a joint setting where the other branches or allied nations may not be as inclined to quickly tend to the needs of their people. When it's possible, and it usually is, be sure your airmen have access to e-mail and phones so they can interact with family back home to announce safe arrival.

When you're in the deployed environment, pace your physical activities to a reasonable extent if at all possible; you don't want to run out of energy or adrenaline before the deployment is over. You'll also need to stay well hydrated as you move about. Be sure to roger up to the "Hooah" or "Oorah" shout when you're down range; junior officers participate with everyone else when its time to load gear or unload it from vehicles and small transport aircraft. Also, if the guys don't sense any objection, they should help lady troops tackle heavy physical tasks. Watch out though, some of those gals have more muscle power than the guys.

The Air Force takes care of its people, no matter where they're deployed. Quality-of-life items (e.g., washers, dryers, TVs) are flowed to forward locations not long after transporting in the weapon systems. But don't rub that in the face of the other services; some resent the fact that the Air Force is so well provisioned with creature comforts and that airmen sometimes stay in hotels instead of tents when deployed. Amenities may even reach an extreme when you're serving with allied nations; a couple of them bring the crystal and silver to the battlefield to ensure that their officers have a proper mess. Nevertheless, you'll end up the winner of any one-upmanship contest once they see the ice cream machine in the dining facility on your airbase.

If and when the environment becomes safe and your base is no longer in "lockdown," take time to occasionally smell the roses while on deployment. Enjoy a desert sunset, visit a local village, tour an archeological site, etc. While on deployment, be sure to purchase some durable artifact that reflects the culture of the geographic area; you'll get a lifetime of enjoyment from having this type of keepsake in your office or home. Be sure your "war trophy" is legal to import back to the U.S., and don't inadvertently purchase a Made in China item from the local market, unless you are actually in China.

An Air Force officer shouldn't look down his pedigree nose at the other branches of military service as though they were second rate. The military is becoming more "purple suit" all the time, and it would be wise to learn a bit of the other services' history and doctrine so that it's easier to "soldier" with them down range. You should appreciate the fact that each branch of the service has its own aviation arm and that they all operate high-tech unmanned aerial vehicles. Furthermore, weapon systems in every branch are evolving to a standoff, fight-by-wireless concept. So you can be sure that the Army and Navy officers serving alongside you in the tactical setting are very smart and capable, and one of them may even be your boss.

Take advantage of various opportunities to visit historic military facilities and battlegrounds during your world travels; those are places such as the Gettysburg battlefield, Verdun on the Western Front, the USS Arizona Memorial, etc. Walking such hallowed ground will surely enrich your warrior spirit. Also, occasionally visit the wounded in military hospitals or the veterans of past wars. They surely deserve some of your warmth and respect; needless to say, recounts of their deeds and courage will be inspiring. From time to time, read one of the many books that chronicle past wars and portray the exploits of great airmen.

Develop an appreciation for the nation's support of the military. Although the public may disagree with some government decisions regarding use of the military instrument of power, they now have great respect for military personnel deployed overseas. Today, the public doesn't read bland dispatches that arrive days after a skirmish; the Information Age gives them a near real-time view of the conflict occurring in the battlespace. Civilian patriots empathize with their fellow Americans who are practicing the art of war, and remotely viewing the hostilities may even be a vicarious experience for some. The military is enjoying a never before seen level of public support, and that's extremely beneficial to all airmen as they go in harm's way.

Be they Christian, Moslem, Jew, or whatever faith, most military officers are "Holy Warriors" in a certain sense and to a certain degree. If you happen to be an agnostic or atheist, everyone must respect your freedom to not choose religion; however, you won't be in true harmony with the vast majority of military personnel who are persons of faith. Plus, you might find yourself disadvantaged by the lack of a spiritual point of reference in your military life, and that's something that can help get a person through the toughest of times. In any case, a godless theology is not prevalent among military leaders. Theoretically, that's not supposed to matter, yet it really does matter in some situations.

The great American philosopher Mark Twain once said, "Courage is resistance to fear, mastery of fear—not the absence of fear." In times of conflict, the natural apprehension of an enemy's fighting capability remains suppressed while one vigorously engages in actions to either counter, neutralize or destroy that capability. Synchronizing with the mindset of key senior officers in a hostile fire zone bolsters one's courage and confidence even further. An Air Force officer must valiantly and zealously lead his airmen in the performance of their assigned roles during the air campaign. You'll most certainly rise to meet that noble challenge, and you can be sure that all your fellow officers are going to do exactly the same; hence, U.S. airpower will always prevail.

Chapter 2
PROFESSIONAL KNOWLEDGE

As an officer, you're surely smart enough to know that you don't know everything, despite the fact that you've just disengaged from more than sixteen grueling years of school. You show up on the scene as a recently commissioned officer who possesses baseline knowledge. Then you proceed to build on that foundation by acquiring more specific knowledge and relevant experience, an activity that must continue throughout your entire officer career. The amalgamation of all that knowledge and experience should constitute wisdom. Hopefully, some of the advice that follows will help you quickly become wise beyond your years.

Actively compete for the chance to attend advanced courses and professional development schools in residence. New types of leadership and management tools are needed in order to meet the increased responsibilities that come with promotion; the schoolhouse is the best place to plus-up your toolbox. Attending those schools should be all about gaining knowledge, not just getting your "ticket punched" to increase chances for promotion. While it's great to "go for the gold," it's better to say focused on the learning experience, rather than on winning academic laurels. That's because graduating with honors is not really a 100 percent guarantee that you're graduating with more smarts.

Officer Professional Development correspondence courses are often characterized as a cross that a young officer must bear. Even so, you need to enroll in the course appropriate to your rank, or participate via the seminar mode. If you don't do those courses, you'll be missing out on important knowledge and you'll fall into disfavor with your boss. Don't put your duties and the rest of your life on hold while doing the courses, just progress at a reasonable and steady pace. However, if you have less than two-thirds of a correspondence program completed and you're officially selected to attend the school in residence, confirm that your commander is going to release you to attend; then immediately withdraw from the correspondence course.

A master's degree enhances your professional standing, and the advanced degree is pretty much a prerequisite for promotion to lieutenant colonel. But do not start pursuing a master's degree until after you pin on captain; that's plenty soon enough to preclude a crash program as you get closer to needing the degree in order to be competitive for further promotion. Set a pace that doesn't hinder your normal duty performance. You could attend classes locally after duty hours or via distance learning on the internet. In either case, check www.chea.org to be sure the school is accredited, pay attention to residency requirements, and major in something that's germane to your military duties.

After disengaging from the academic environment, apply your newly acquired knowledge in a practical manner that's relevant to the reality of the operating environment. Stay current in your specific career field so that you'll clearly understand as your people articulate their innovations, challenges and achievements. If you don't "get it," they'll see a disheartening "deer-in-the-headlights" expression on your face. If you discover that you've got a knowledge shortfall, capitalize on computer-based training or webcast seminars to get quickly spun up in a specific area. For example, a logistics officer might need to get smart on machine-to-machine communications, a new technology that's going to revolutionize the tracking of in-transit cargo.

No matter what their career field is, all officers need to acquire a general knowledge of information technology (IT); that's because systems and networks are the enablers for a host of military capabilities that cut across all disciplines. Even the older flag officers have acquired IT savvy, particularly in light of the fact that cyberspace is the Air Force's newest war-fighting domain. Contemporary warfighters utilize mission planning systems fed by fused sensors, and all the elements are widely distributed across secure data networks. And the "trigger-pullers" now operate from standoff locations, reaching out through cyberspace to launch and guide surgical air strikes. In fact, IT finally gives the "good guys" an edge in asymmetrical warfare.

Routinely read one monthly periodical that's related to your career field. That will keep you generally aware of recent developments in the commercial world, some of which may be applicable to your unit and the Air Force mission. You'll also want to establish a rich site summary (RSS) feed on your desktop computer in order to receive a personally tailored flow of information that's relevant to your specific career field. The occasional one-day seminar is another good way to keep up with advancements in your career field, and web-based technology makes it possible to have a virtual presence at some of those events.

Gain a basic understanding of current management issues and trends, such as Change Management, and Six Sigma. You may ask yourself, "Does a successful precision air strike on a terrorist target constitute topnotch customer service?" Yes it does, for everyone but the terrorist. There are many cascading processes and services leading up to the actual airstrike. Management consultants are bent on optimizing those processes for the military. However, look to your boss for signals as to how deeply he wants you to get involved in such programs. You wouldn't want to get drawn deeply into an exuberant consultant's program and then find out that your boss only "signed up" for cursory participation. Although, you can anticipate that your boss will be keen on Air Force Smart Operations for the Twenty-first Century.

The Air Force has transformed its regulations into sets of instructions. Learn their general structure so that you can quickly research them online. There's no need to actually memorize any of them, but do get very familiar with the ones that are relevant to your primary duties. In the same vein, there's an old cliché that says, "Regulations were made to be broken." That twisted rationale was heresy in a culture that mandated blind compliance. But today's policies and instructions are a little bit broader, and therefore do offer a degree of sensible latitude. In fact, any policy that impedes mission-oriented activity ought to be questioned from time to time; it may be in need of updating, or may even have become obsolete.

Learn how to read financial statements and manpower documents, and understand the mechanics of a cost-benefit analysis. You need to do this because resources are so tight that you'll end up competing with your peers to get what you need to do the job: personnel, funding, real estate, etc. Yes, the "bean counters" will consume your time and energy by having you prove over and over why you still need what is clearly the absolute minimum manpower and funding to get the job done. However, the positive spinoff is that during the analysis, you may discover a more efficient production process or a better way to employ your existing manpower.

Today, many of the military's support functions and services are being handled by civilian contractors, even in hostile fire zones. Learn at least the basic elements of contracting so that you can have productive interactions with experts involved in your outsourcing or procurement actions. They'll often expect you to draft a request for proposal or statement of work for the contract you want established. It's equally important that you be able to perceive when contractors are performing properly or when they might be shortchanging you and the government. Defense contractors, many of whom are military veterans, will be much more inclined to do their jobs well when they realize that you're smart on the essentials of contract monitoring.

Even though you're a warrior at heart, you'll still have to learn to touch-type at a high speed. During your Air Force career, your hands will be on a keyboard and a mouse much more than you could possibly imagine. That skill isn't just for when you tackle your many literary endeavors. Intelligence, surveillance, reconnaissance, and target strikes are being increasingly conducted via the computer keyboard, mouse, and joystick. In fact, you may as well add the video game controller to that group of peripherals. However, don't expect to be awarded a Purple Heart if you develop carpal tunnel syndrome while engaged in point-and-click warfare.

Develop your computer graphics skills to the point where you can at least create basic slides and modify existing slides on your own. If your briefing is going to be presented in another organization's facilities, be sure to e-mail a copy to your host's staff and also bring a copy on a CD. Due to security risks, you'll probably be barred from using a thumb-drive. When it comes time to present the briefing, remember to provide a hard copy set of slides, with space for the dignitary to make notes. Never brag about your computer graphics skills lest you find yourself becoming the staff's briefing slide guru and webmaster. You want to avoid being tagged as a professional "PowerPoint Ranger"; that's not a legitimate occupation for an officer.

Learn about the host country prior to an overseas assignment. In order to operate amongst the indigenous population, you'll need to be sensitive to their social norms, unique behavior, and religious practices. The book *Kiss, Bow or Shake Hands* by Morrison, Conaway, and Borden provides a quick primer for sixty different countries. It's also important to learn the country's geography and topology. Immerse yourself in the country's culture when you get there, but don't get too carried away when going native unless you're actually assigned as an International Affairs Specialist. Never forget who you are when you're with the local nationals, whether it's for military business or social activity.

Become fully proficient in one other language. Mandarin, Arabic, and Russian are among the good choices. If you've already studied a foreign language, take it to the next level of proficiency. These days, it's easy to stay fully immersed in a foreign language via internet newspapers (www.thepaperboy.com), web-based TV and radio, and satellite TV broadcasts. When overseas, you may occasionally find yourself in a situation where the host nation officers speak English and fellow U.S. officers traveling with you do not speak the foreign language. To avoid an awkward situation, initially converse with the hosts in the foreign language, and then switch to English. Everyone will admire your bilingual talent, and they'll appreciate your sensitivity.

Own a copy of the *Guide to AF Protocol*, the *Blue Book of Etiquette*, and the *Air Force Officer's Guide* so that you'll always have protocol information at your fingertips. Jump at the chance to serve as project officer for the hosting of a Distinguished Visitor's stay with your unit. You'll find it to be an enriching experience, and your boss will be grateful to you. But run the other way fast if anyone ever asks you to become a protocol officer as a full-time job. There's a tongue-in-cheek joke that says protocol officers are all fired into their jobs, a rather cynical quip that has a small element of truth to it. One of the spinoff benefits of hosting a dignitary is enjoying a fine dining event; in fact, a true hedonist might even claim that he's proud to eat for his country.

It's imperative that all officers memorize the words to the national anthem, the Air Force song, and the oath of enlistment; and you should eventually add the commissioning oath of office to your repertoire. There will be countless ceremonies and events where you'll express those hallowed words, and it's really poor form to read them from them a "cheat sheet" or from the back of a dining-in program. Your troops and officers will be highly inspired by your sincerity and strength as you look them in the eye while they repeat the oath that you confidently recite from memory.

Know the procedures for properly displaying the American flag; this includes both indoor and outdoor settings. Step in and correct those situations where the flag is not being properly displayed or when proper courtesies are not being rendered. However, don't take that corrective action in a manner that would publicly humiliate an individual who was momentarily distracted or was ignorant of the proper procedures. Publicly "going off" in someone's face just builds up fear and resentment; what you really want to do is instill and foster patriotism.

Chapter 3
PURPOSEFUL PRESENCE

As an officer, you should have some control over your daily activities. However, it's difficult to meet all the many commitments that arise, particularly when you're trying to accomplish even more despite continually decreasing resources, time being one of them. You just can't be in all places all the time; you'd simply burn yourself out in a futile attempt to be physically present everywhere you're invited or expected to be. Fortunately, there are numerous tactics you can employ to make your presence more pervasive, with greater efficiency.

Don't spend your day bouncing around as though you were trapped inside a pinball machine. At the end of each duty day, quickly plan out a simple and efficient schedule of activity for the next duty day. Print those appointments on a small card and carry it with you, or load the appointments into your "PDA" palmtop computer. Don't constantly call for staff meetings, and don't let yourself get drawn into all meetings, briefings and ceremonies. Instead, only say yes to the ones that are relevant to your duties, position and professional relationships, and gently say no to those that aren't relevant.

Do not receive everyone who wants to interact with you; your time management efforts will go straight down the tubes. Have an open door policy but don't let people take unfair advantage of that privilege. If the visitor is an enlisted troop who keeps going around his supervisor to directly interact with you on routine matters, you'll have to ask him if he gave his boss an opportunity to work the issue. Sometimes it might be more appropriate for a visitor to meet with someone who works for you or with you, a person who is closer to the issue at hand. The inverse is also true; walk amongst your people often enough so that they're able to sense your continuous presence without having to personally witness you sitting behind your walnut desk.

If you have an issue or resource at stake in a meeting or at a conference, be there to defend it or count on losing the battle to the officer who at least manifested an interest in the outcome. When you're called upon to speak to an issue, your passion will be appreciated but it will only carry you so far. You have to be able to articulate an objective and convincing argument to win support for your position, and you have to do it without whining and without taking cheap shots at opposing parties. You might even have to campaign hard to ensure that increasingly austere resources remain dedicated to your existing projects and programs. In any event, be present in order to protect your slice of the resource pie.

Review your contact list before you head out to a meeting so that you'll immediately recognize the attendees and know their names. Show up for appointments and meetings five minutes early so that you'll be able to network a bit with peers and superiors. Have lunch in the military mess or officers club two or three times a week, rather than frequenting fast-food joints or "brown-bagging" your lunch. You'll achieve a more visible presence at the club, and you're likely to have some meaningful interaction with fellow officers. Maybe you'll even have healthier and better tasting food.

Minimize costly long distance travel; instead, utilize the various voice and video conferencing capabilities that were once exclusively reserved for very senior officers. This is particularly applicable once you've actually met the meeting participants in person at least one time. From that point on, there is almost no additional benefit to a physical meeting as opposed to some form of telepresence. Furthermore, virtual meetings on desktop computers are now possible via the military version of the internet, in both the secure and non-secure modes. Virtual meetings save your unit a great deal of travel money and save you travel time, some of which could constitute quality time with your family and friends.

Occasionally (not frequently) visit your 24/7 work centers at night; it shows your airmen that you care about them and appreciate their sacrifice of being up while the rest of the world sleeps. Be curious during your visit but don't make it an inspection event that causes your people to pray that you never come around again. When the airmen are showing you a piece of equipment or a system, let them do almost all the talking so they can proudly impress you with their knowledge. Remain sensitive to the fact that a shift worker's break is the same as your weekend; although, sometimes you just can't avoid calling them in for meetings. Also, get a small team together to cater food and snacks to the shift workers stuck in your work centers on Thanksgiving and Christmas Day.

Attend at least the key sporting events that your organization participates in; your people will notice and appreciate your presence. Be enthusiastic while in the stands, but don't loudly "bad-mouth" the competing team. By the way, when serving overseas, it's traditional to make duty schedule adjustments so the troops can enjoy the Super Bowl on a real-time basis in the middle of the night. The satellite broadcast of the football game is usually shown on the big briefing screen in an organization's conference room so that a large group can enjoy the game together; again, this smart rule-bending is only done at overseas locations. Perhaps the Indy 500 also merits some rule-bending—your call.

You can prioritize official ceremonies and social events, attending the most important ones, making an appearance at some of them, and sending "regrets" for the others. Consider your spouse or girlfriend in this; some of those events could constitute an evening out on the town. This is particularly true if there's a military ceremony involved or if the event is being held at some spectacular location, which frequently happens during overseas assignments. In other words, it's possible to get "double duty" out of an obligatory event by encouraging your spouse to savor some of the more dramatic events and opulent settings with you.

When you're at a civic function, military ceremony, or social event, your presence will be more obvious if you mingle with other attendees and guests rather than getting into extended chitchat with only one or two persons for the duration of the event. Some of the more experienced party hostesses will literally prod a guest who stays locked onto another guest for too long. On the other hand, if flirting is one of your favorite sports, just remember that the party is a goldfish bowl where everyone's actions are highly visible, particularly to the senior military officers who may be present.

If your troops invite you to a social event, they're simply being nice to you. They neither expect nor do they want you to remain present all the way through to the end of the party. When you first arrive, it's probably smart to interact with your more senior folks first so they can audibly address you as Lieutenant or Captain. If you approach the less seasoned troops first, one of them may be caught up in the spirit (or spirits) of the party and address you by your first name, which you must immediately but gracefully correct them on. Accept an "adult beverage" so that partygoers won't feel uncomfortable about drinking in your presence; however, nurse the drink and don't get conned into overindulging.

Meet the spouses of your troops during unit gatherings so that you can talk up the military member's mission-related contributions and achievements. Such insights will mean a lot to the family and will probably cause the spouse to be more supportive of the military member's career. Actually, hosting an open house day for families is a smart investment of your time. The spouse who understands the unit's mission and appreciates the big role her mate plays in it will share in the unit's pride and be supportive of the mission. Exactly the opposite will happen if the spouse is left in the dark while the military member spends long hours on duty.

When your troops are sick in the hospital, visit them at least once if their stay is short and several times if their stay is long. Make sure that a unit member or spouse stays in continual contact with the hospitalized individual's family to help them obtain support or services, particularly at overseas locations. If that connection is not maintained, a very loud and embarrassing alarm bell will go off in public as the family mistakenly perceives themselves to be abandoned by their boss and associates. Also, make sure the commander and the first sergeant know when one of your troops is in the hospital.

Always take or make time to meet with the chaplain when he visits your branch or flight, and extend all the appropriate courtesies and amenities. The chaplain is not a superfluous entity, even if he's of a different faith than you. He'll stimulate and enrich the atmosphere when he visits your team. Most of your troops will appreciate the booster shot of spiritual strength the chaplain provides, particularly in deployed settings. Also, keep in mind that command chaplains usually brief their generals upon return to the headquarters, reporting on the health of the unit and citing the strongest leaders—you're one of them!

Chapter 4
IMAGE PROJECTION

The stereotype of an Air Force officer is essentially a cross between Gregory Peck in the movie *Twelve O'clock High* and Will Smith in *Independence Day*. Even though you may pretty much fit that glamorous mold, most Air Force officers possess and project a more personal image that's based on innate qualities, instilled values, and learned behavior. In the end, all of that melds to form the real you, operating in your role as a commissioned officer wearing the blue suit. Here's some advice you may want to consider as you begin to walk amongst your fellow airmen as a proud Air Force officer.

Leading the charge with a bottle in one hand and a sword in the other is a practice that ended with the passing of John Wayne. But strong leaders still have some degree of charisma and flamboyance. Some are characterized as rock stars, others as all-star quarterbacks, and there might even be few warrior princesses out there. That's all wonderful, but do keep in mind that there's a fine line between confidence and arrogance; don't let your head get too far into the clouds. Also, you can occasionally operate like a raging bull, or even a pit bull with lipstick; just be aware that the people cleaning up all the "broken glass" left in your path will probably consider you just another bull in the china closet.

Be self-confident without being focused on yourself, and avoid becoming smug or pompous. Being in the profession of arms is certainly serious business, but it's also supposed to be fun in the grand scheme of things; so it's OK to smile once in awhile. Also, display good posture and stay conscious of your body language; it can emphasize what you're saying or deliver an entirely different message. Most everyone is a little bit rough around the edges in some areas; just be the best and most genuine edition of yourself, and you'll eventually win everyone's respect.

It's good to lighten up from time to time, at the right time. But never be humorous in a way that degrades or humiliates others, or even yourself for that matter. In other words, don't be afraid to laugh at yourself but never intentionally make yourself the butt of your own joke. Even though inadvertently locking yourself out of your car last week may seem to be a hugely comical situation in retrospect, keep it to yourself and preserve your dignity. Of course, officers never try to impress others by telling off-color jokes; to do so would shock most of the listeners and would certainly offend many of them. Also keep in mind that when you're down range, there will be some moments when there's no room for any humor at all.

There are still the few odd commissioned officers who tend to put on airs and act snobby. It's one thing for your chest to swell with pride, but don't let your ego overinflate just because of your rank and position; you are a human leading other humans. If you put yourself on a pedestal, folks won't do anything to keep you from falling off of it. However, if they put you on that pedestal, they'll do anything and everything to make sure you stay up there. When you sense that happening, you can be pretty sure you've won the trust, loyalty and admiration of your troops.

Officers display confidence and a positive attitude no matter what the circumstances. Your demeanor will instill enthusiasm and optimism in your subordinates as the team is facing significant challenges. Be sure you have your bearings and that you've set the smartest course to the common goal; then have faith that the airmen on the team you're leading will bring about a positive outcome. They'll be checking you for signs of your own self-confidence and your confidence in them; that alone can go a long way towards inspiring them to charge forward in the face of some pretty challenging circumstances.

As an officer, you need to manifest your strong conviction when you're working a serious issue. Get focused and show a bit of fire in your eyes when you're dialoguing with the enlisted troops; they need to be excited and enthusiastic about what you're telling them to do. At the same time, make sure they understand that the feedback channel to you is always open, without inviting frivolous arguments. Also, when you're meeting with people in your office, keep your chair level up a bit higher than the level your visitors are sitting at. Although chair height may seem to be an extremely trivial matter, just take it as being a significant ergonomics issue.

Never lose your temper in public; however, a smattering of carefully controlled anger at just the right moment, in just the right setting, can energize the atmosphere and move people to action. An example would be frequent performance problems in some area of production. In a closed door staff meeting you might consciously reveal a bit of your pent-up frustration and loudly say, "This disturbing trend is going to stop, and I mean right now..." Perhaps you even slam your fist on the top of your desk for emphasis. The natural reaction of those in attendance is to fix whatever has the boss so riled up. Bear in mind that such psychological tactics are only effective if they're reserved for rare occasions.

Officers are not lethargic; stay fit so that you'll feel and emanate energy. Opt for an elliptical trainer when outdoor running isn't possible; treadmills and Wii Fit systems just aren't enough. The elliptical trainer is easy on the joints, the upper body gets a workout, and there's no vehicle traffic to contend with. You're not excused from this when you're TDY; soft street shoes, shorts and a tee shirt can pass for workout togs in a hotel gym. Also, some of the hotels you'll stay at have an indoor pool as a fitness option. Above all, don't let your subconscious mind trick you into staying stuck behind the desk to avoid regular exercise—"I just can't break away from all this paperwork." Invigorating physical activity will improve your productivity and your stamina.

Just as you take care of your physical health, you also need to optimize your psychological health. Don't become a victim of self-generated stress, and avoid getting caught up needlessly in irrational self-doubt. If your stress were to become chronic, you could experience physiological manifestations. The remedy is to break the cycle of stress. If you slip into the workaholic lifestyle, come up for air once in awhile. Get revitalized by engaging in outdoor activity, attending a sporting event, or visiting with cheerful friends. Take a mini-vacation from time to time, doing something other than catching up on chores around the house. Bottom line is, stay focused on the positive side of life and adopt a work hard, play hard ethic.

Participate on a unit sports team if you enjoy playing a particular sport. All eyes will be upon you; therefore, opt for those sports in which you're at least a competent and competitive performer. If you're a great tennis player, get on the court and show your stuff. But if you're a proven klutz on the softball field, don't stand out there and miss fly balls in front of everyone. Don't play sports so hard that you push yourself way beyond your physical limits, and don't participate in dangerous "extreme" sports. You have to be able to fully perform your duties the day after a sporting event, and you must stay fit for worldwide duty. The battle scars you receive while in the sports arena will only win your boss's sympathy, not his admiration.

Officers cannot look all haggard and ragged, no matter how physically demanding the activity, on duty or off duty. Recover at the first opportunity if you get sweaty, sloppy and exhausted. Take a brief time-out, enjoy a quick shower, don fresh attire, and then reengage. By the way, three uniforms of a given type may be considered standard issue, but an officer always needs to have a couple of extra uniforms of each type at the ready. One other thing about grooming: clipping your nails while you're meeting with someone is unacceptable behavior, at least until you make full colonel. Similarly, don't rest your feet on top of your desk until you become a general.

Install a full-length mirror at home and in your office; check yourself when leaving home and before meetings. Keep extra rank and insignia clips (frogs) on hand. Place an extra hat with rank on it in your office, and carry it in your briefcase when you travel. Stow a roll of masking tape in your desk so that it's available to pat lint or pet hair off of your uniform. Keep a pair of small scissors close at hand for trimming loose threads off of your uniforms. Also, find a shop or tailor that can provide the equivalent of an Air Force tie to replace the tacky version that was issued to you and is also sold in military clothing stores.

Tailor your uniform so that it fits right; a slightly stocky person looks like a "porker" in a uniform that's too tight. If you gain a bit of weight, buy the next size up and then have the uniform tailored to fit properly. If you didn't get a loose-fitting mess dress, be aware that you'll soon start to outgrow the one you have: first the trousers, then the jacket, and then finally the cummerbund as you approach twenty years of military service. When this morphing starts, some desperate officers resort to linking two mess dress chains in order to create one elongated chain big enough to close the front of their jacket. Buying new uniform items that fit right and feel comfortable is the better solution.

The goal while in uniform is to look very smart and highly professional, not sexually alluring. Don't get carried away with the cologne or perfume; your fellow airmen in the work center or aboard the aircraft will get dizzy just being around you. Female officers should certainly wear makeup if they wish, but not to the point of being preposterous. For example, false eyelashes might be a bit extreme. And male officers really shouldn't wear a mustache even though they're authorized to do so. In short, it's best for on-duty officers to set the glamour threshold at a point where they present a striking image, within the context of military professionalism.

Don't wear gaudy jewelry or an excess of jewelry. You want people to interact with you, not stare at the bright turquoise and silver bracelet you picked up during your last trip out west. Also, it doesn't make any sense for ladies to wear diamond earrings when dressed in the battle uniform. Some airmen depend on a complex multifunction watch while on duty; others get along fine with just a simple watch. In any event, a very elegant and dressy watch that has roman numerals or simple marks for the hours is going to be very difficult to read during hectic operations, and it may be incompatible with the duty uniform.

Everyone wears essentially the same uniform, so your hair style automatically becomes a prominent feature of your personal appearance. Hair style should conform to military standards and not be a trendy, unorthodox cut. What's it going to be? High and tight, short Afro, parted down the middle (perhaps not), or shaved head? Visualize the image you'll present to your fellow airmen, or actually check it out via some fancy computer software. Once you're comfortable with the new image, visit the hair stylist for the real deal. You might even have to go off base to find a competent hair stylist. Some older male officers color away gray hair, but there's no reason for a young company grade male officer to color his hair. Bleached blond male CGOs just make their bosses see red.

These days, the human body is subject to all kinds of decorations and alterations. Tattoos on officers are absolutely taboo. Don't get one if you don't have one now, and get rid of your tattoo if you do have one. Synthetic ink can be lased off without too much difficulty and expense. Air Force ladies should never have their lips pumped up to an extreme by some fly-by-night cosmetic surgeon; exaggerated and poorly executed lip enhancements look absolutely bizarre. An officer should do everything in moderation, including eating properly and getting regular exercise to stay toned up and in shape. Resorting to last-ditch tactics such as liposuction and prescription drugs to meet weight standards is outrageous and dangerous.

Your college fraternity and sorority days are over. Officers shouldn't run around in public places wearing blue jeans, T-shirts, and sweat shirts. If you absolutely must wear blue jeans, make sure they're high-end designer jeans, or wear black or beige jeans. Never, ever wear "sawed-off" jeans as shorts or walk around in public wearing flip-flops. At the O'Club, the gentlemen usually wear a sport coat (even if it's without a tie) and the ladies should wear attire on a similar level in the evening. The lady officers might opt to dress in the most contemporary styles, but the attire should be tastefully conservative in terms of what gets emphasized or exposed.

You'll require dressy civilian attire for some social events, particularly when in Washington, D.C., or overseas. Your wardrobe should include a dark blue or black business suit (equivalent for ladies), plus a blazer and a low-key sport coat. Don't waste money on expensive tailor-made suits unless you're independently wealthy. "Off-the-rack" attire is just fine if it's high quality and altered for an optimum fit. Polyester is totally unacceptable unless it's a poly/wool blend. Gaudy and very bright ties look bad; always wear a tie clasp. Wear black shoes, not brown, with dark blue or black suits. A medium-weight topcoat will be needed, preferably water repellant with zip-out lining.

When you're assigned overseas, you'll occasionally be in the company of local nationals in various settings. Things are a bit more formal over there in terms of attire, and you'll notice that in many countries your local national counterparts wear their service dress uniform on a daily basis. When attire isn't indicated on an invitation or you're in doubt about what to wear, call the secretary of the senior officer or host to find out what is suitable for the occasion at hand. Sporty clothing such as T-shirts, shorts and athletic shoes are not usually worn by international officers at social events or in fine restaurants. Also, loud and boisterous behavior in restaurants and cafes is not appreciated by the locals; besides, it's smart for an officer to maintain a low profile as an antiterrorist measure.

Eliminate clutter in your office, and paint dingy or dirty walls. If you choose to have a few plants, stick to high quality artificial plants that are maintenance-free. Don't load up the office with cutesy knickknacks that don't have anything to do with the military culture. However, some action photo of you in a big sports moment would add to the décor of the office: football, skiing, sky-diving, etc. Make at least one major improvement to the office during your tenure, such as new carpeting, a bookcase, etc. Funds are tight, so the cleaning service is mostly reserved for the very senior officers; you'll probably have to tidy up your own office or cubicle during your off-duty time.

You'll occasionally be asked what your "go-by" name is. Come up with or accept a dignified "call sign"; for example, Captain Robert "Reflex" Jones, the fighter pilot, or Captain

Stephanie "Striker" Curtis, the combat systems officer. Maybe a nickname like Lieutenant Rockford "Rocky" Smith has worked for you all the way from your school days. No matter how you acquire it, make sure the name is sensible and somehow relevant to you. Your fellow officers, and at times your boss, will address you by that name. It makes you a bit more personable and colorful as an officer. In case you were wondering, "SpongeBob" has already been taken by a field grade officer.

Your signature is a small but important aspect of your image. Readers formulate an impression of you based on your signature even if it only happens at a subconscious level. If your signature looks sloppy or crude, consider refining it by adding some style and flair. Many great persons in history had impressive signatures; some were legible and some were not. If your signature is illegible, there should at least be some visual relationship between your spelled name and your flamboyant signature. Also, it would be rather audacious for a company grade officer to sign a document by making a single illegible squiggle, as do some flag officers who have certainly earned the right to enjoy a small degree of arrogance.

Choose a businesslike ring tone for your cell phone, rather than a movie theme or a hip-hop chant that creates a spectacle. You're authorized to wear a cell phone on the uniform belt; however, if your phone is slim and small, it looks much better to carry it in a pocket. Avoid wearing a Blue-Tooth earpiece except when it's needed for hands-free driving. If you have a military cell phone, don't make personal calls within earshot of others unless you have unlimited calling, and then only use it for urgent matters generally related to your duties. "Honey, we're working a hot issue here, so I won't get home until about seven o'clock."

An officer really shouldn't commute to the base in a rusty old pickup truck that has a crude woodshed bolted onto the bed. Actually, officers shouldn't drive dilapidated automobiles or the cheapest models available. Show at least a modicum of pride by driving a clean and well appointed car, even if it's many years old. When you choose your next car, pick a make and model that can be serviced where you next expect to be assigned overseas. Your car always needs to be in excellent mechanical condition because it transports you to your duty location each day, and sometimes to the hotspot of a local emergency with your boss in the passenger seat!

The old movie *Dr. Strangelove* depicts Strategic Air Command back in the day. In it, a B-52 aircrew commander descended into the bomb bay and mounted a nuke as though it were a wild horse; then he rode it straight down to the enemy target—pretty extreme showmanship! That sort of stunt is probably out of the question for you; however, some sensible showmanship on your part will convince your troops that their leader isn't some stuffy bureaucrat. If your technicians maintain microwave radio antennas, climb to the top of the tower with them to view their work up there. If your troops maintain a C-130 gunship, see if you can get aboard to fire the Gatling gun on the range. Otherwise; become a champion skeet shooter, get into scuba diving, etc.

Traditionally, the rated officers wearing leather jackets and flight suits are slightly arrogant and cocky, or at least display extraordinary self-confidence. It's not at all surprising that "stick jockeys" and aircrew members walk with a bit of a swagger. After all, they're more closely associated with the flying mission aloft than are the officers who fill important support roles on the ground. However, officers should avoid two potential extremes: the superiority complex and the inferiority complex. There has to be mutual respect amongst all airmen because, in one way or another, each member of the Air Force team is proudly contributing to the success of airpower.

Chapter 5
DYNAMIC LEADERSHIP

When a gemstone is being polished, is beauty being created or is it being revealed? That's the essence of the perennial question, "Are leaders born or are they made?" The answer is, both. Strong leadership is a combination of innate talent and learned skills, and the balance of those two factors is not necessarily the same in equally successful leaders. Success as an Air Force officer is all about leadership. It doesn't matter whether you're an aviator, a technocrat or a bureaucrat; you'll ultimately have to show the way ahead, orchestrate required resources, and motivate your airmen. In the end, mission success will result from the collective achievements of the people you've inspired and led. Here are a few ideas on the subject.

The word "subordinate" may imply inferiority; however, recruiters aren't bringing "blank slates" into today's Air Force. The newly arrived raw troops are actually contemporary adults who possess a fair degree of academic and social sophistication, and these natural born citizens of the digital world are primed to use high-tech weapons and to fight in cyberspace. Most Air Force enlisted personnel quickly earn their associates degree, and many of the senior NCOs have a bachelor's degree. Your subordinates are today's military professionals, and they're bound to develop a sense of pride under your strong leadership.

An Air Force leader needs to foster a winning team that's passionate about achieving mission objectives. Understand and be sensitive to the psyche of your group, playing up the commonality of its members and downplaying their differences. Peer pressure will begin to emerge as individuals start melding into a single team under your leadership. There'll be mutual respect and reinforcement amongst the solid performers, and the informal leaders will shun the few persons who refuse to contribute to the group's success. None of this will seem to be happening at the onset, but the effect will become apparent as critical mass is achieved.

Lead your people rather than boss them. An overbearing boss orders and intimidates subordinates so that they'll achieve specific results. But if that method is carried too far or is continuous, the team will only do exactly what they're told to do, only when they're told to do it. That's not leadership; it's micromanagement of humans who are being treated as mere tools. An infallible genius who has total situational awareness and unlimited energy can achieve success by bossing people in that manner. However, that authoritarian methodology will result in failure if the boss loses focus for even a brief period. Furthermore, the boss's own personal limitations will set a ceiling on his team's performance, and his uninspired troops won't grow to their full potential.

Your airmen want and need a strong leader who serves as a point of reference and source of direction for them, particularly in this era of rapid change. That doesn't mean you have to figure everything out for yourself. You'll find participative management to be appropriate in many situations, as long everyone knows that you're the leader who gives the final green light. However, in chaotic situations, you'll tend to lead in a more forceful manner so that the way ahead is clear to everyone and so that your people stay fully committed to your team's goals.

Your people shouldn't be afraid to bring you bad news; there are some things you've just got to know about right away. Above all, don't shoot the messenger. Keep in mind that the bearer of bad news may be in an elevated state of anxiety, both because of the bad news he bears and because he's the one bearing it. Be calm and reassuring as you absorb the facts and contemplate a course of action. Then get out from behind your desk and visit the site of the crisis in order to better understand the situation. Work with your senior NCOs and fellow officers to find an immediate solution to remedy the situation, including a permanent fix for the root cause.

You must get more than just a good effort from your airmen; sweat and fatigue alone do not bring forth adequate results. If need be, break a huge, complex job down into tasks that can be accomplished sequentially. Or it could be that a few of your people need a quick dose of specialized training to maintain production equipment that's new to the inventory. Perhaps some on-call technical support should be brought into play. Maybe some resource is needed, like extra vehicles to expedite the movement of materials. In any case, you must continually encourage your people, ensure their efforts are focused in the right direction, and provide them with a clear view of progress towards the feasible goal that they've committed to achieving.

Once in a long while, one of your capable people will get psychologically stuck in the mud while working a task. When this occurs, don't let him use you as a sounding board to talk himself out of success. First, ascertain that he has all the required resources and training to do the job. Then express your confidence in his ability to get the job done, and get him to commit to reengaging with enthusiasm and vigor. You may even have to employ some mild form of shock therapy to jump-start the stalled individual, just don't resort to a kick-start approach. Once the job gets done, you'll observe the person's surprise at his own ability to overcome the psychological obstacle, and the surprise will quickly evolve into a sense of pride.

There will be times when you have to ask your troops to do the impossible. If they believe in you and trust you, they'll do whatever it takes to get the job done. Just make sure that what you're asking them to do is directly related to the mission, with no hidden agenda. Never ask them to do something that's primarily focused on your own career progression or personal benefit. Your troops will do anything for you once they begin to understand that your aims are truly noble and support the collective well-being of the military organization.

Your people can't continuously operate in the "above and beyond" mode. They'll burn out if they carry on like that for too long, and your team must have enough energy left to go the full distance. Stimulate your people to their maximum performance level at just the right time, not all the time. It's up to you to determine exactly when the team needs to "ramp up" to meet the next challenge. Be sure to organize the proper recognition and reward for the team leaders after the fact; perhaps you could even extend some subtle form of recognition to the informal leader.

When you order people to do something, your top concern must be their safety. You'll be held accountable if they're injured on duty. And if they're injured off duty or commit a Driving Under the Influence (DUI) violation, you'll be asked if the right things were done to have prevented the accident: holiday safety briefings, 101 Critical Days briefing, designated driver program, etc. Be careful about providing a case of beer to the team after everyone becomes dehydrated playing sports in the hot sun; a person in that state gets a buzz from just one or two beers.

Always provide a cooler of soft drinks as an alternative beverage, and make sure those beer drinkers have their feet back on the ground before they start driving.

The enlisted troops might test you when you first show up as a company grade officer, particularly as a second lieutenant. They'll unveil some particularly sticky problem for you to deal with or watch as you face your first big decision. There's no malice intended; they just want to see what stuff you're made of. Remember that your rank and authority allow you to tell them what to do. You're in charge and should be confident enough to make the call in straightforward situations, and you can trust your own instincts up to a certain point. But common sense should prevent you from making shoot-from-the-hip decisions without the facts, many of which you obtain from or via your troops.

Your people will occasionally approach you with their set of solutions to a given problem, with one solution already identified as the optimum. They may just want the green light to go ahead with what they are sure is the best course of action. Don't view their initiative as somehow diminishing your control; simply give them approval if their solution is in synch with the bigger picture and contributes to mission success. In fact, you should make it clear that you expect them to propose feasible solutions whenever they bring a problem to you, rather than you having to devise all the solutions yourself.

When making decisions, solicit input from your troops and then keep an open mind regarding the various courses of action they offer. Sometimes their input will be about doing things smarter instead of harder, and that's OK too. When you must stick with the original course of action, be sure to express appreciation for the input you've received. When you do order the troops to maintain a given course, your rapport with the more experienced senior NCOs has to be good enough that they'll warn you if you're unwittingly sending the train over a cliff.

Don't delay a difficult decision just because it's a tough call to make; conversely, don't rush a difficult decision just for the purpose of appearing decisive. When possible, delay announcing your decision until the facts and conditions are completely clear. You might appear ambivalent if you routinely end up changing rushed decisions. On the other hand, you can't stubbornly stick to a decision even though the initial circumstances have drastically changed. Stubbornly sticking to a decision may satisfy your pride in the short term, but it could spell disaster in the long run. Whenever the situation allows, explain the rationale for a decision, the expected outcome, and any anticipated side effects.

Stay alert when you first walk into new organizational settings. You may notice some big problem that people have been living with for a long time; maybe they've even habituated on it. Get focused and make the needed improvements smartly and quickly. Examples are: replacement of an outdated machine that keeps breaking down, or refurbishing a "hell-hole" work center so that it becomes a place where the troops are proud to perform their duties. Everyone will take notice of the miracle you made happen, and that can set a positive tone for a long time. Also, don't despair if you're put in charge of a broken-down unit. Up will be the only direction things can go, and you'll be the one leading your branch or flight as it gloriously rises from the ashes.

Sometimes you'll need a sledgehammer to bust through the bureaucracy. Picture the young captain who wanted to eliminate a wall that was separating two very closely associated work centers. Formal requests to do the project were moving through an agonizingly slow approval process. After one too many reports of no progress, he checked to be absolutely certain he wasn't dealing with a load-bearing wall; he stuck a cigar between his teeth, grabbed a sledgehammer, stormed past cowering secretaries, and then smashed a huge opening in the wall to create a portal. The civil engineers were rather peeved at the captain, but his bold approach got results and sent a clear message to everyone, including his own people. Of course, the cigar is optional.

Tasking tends to take the path of least resistance and often goes to the person most likely to deliver success. Consider all members of your team when you're assigning work to your people. Challenge the few low-profile personnel who are holding out; they'll learn to stop wasting energy evading tasks, and they'll start delivering and enjoying success. The real reward for you is when you see the odd slacker start beaming with pride and winning the respect of his peers because he did a real fine job and finally carried his fair share of the load.

Delegate wisely and carefully so that the right people are doing the work you oversee; by doing so, you'll be setting your airmen up for success. You'll delegate a function and the associated authority, but you're still ultimately responsible for the overall outcome. When you're explaining a missed deadline or poor product to your boss, you simply can't put the blame on the troop who dropped the ball. By the same token, don't try to fix every "broke" situation for your troops; give them guidance and resources so they can make the actual fix themselves, which is a true learning experience.

Make change a part of your leadership strategy; that is, deal with transformation in a way that makes you and your people the agents of change instead of the victims of change. You understand the mission, you have the resources, and your people are eager to follow you into a bright future. Devise ways to make the mandated changes work in your favor, and make occasional course corrections as necessary. Always set an upbeat and optimistic tone so that your airmen will sense that the changing times are exciting times.

Stay on the alert for the potential saboteur when you're making large-scale enhancements or big changes in your branch or flight. You may have to reassign a naysayer who is trying to undermine your efforts, especially if it's a disgruntled airman who tries to convert others into becoming skeptics, or even rebels. A person who continually spews negativity might simply be a square peg erroneously placed in a round hole; just moving the person to a more appropriate position somewhere else in your organization may bring about amazing changes in his attitude and performance.

In an environment of constant change and diminishing resources, it will be necessary to take calculated risks from time to time. You'll encourage your people to think outside the box, and then you'll have to follow through and implement some of their smart but unorthodox ideas. If the attempt to implement some clever innovation blows up on the launch pad, don't execute the person who invented the idea. Get him to modify his concept or put him in charge of another initiative that's destined for success. In addition, when you decide to take risks, try to organize things so that you're the only person facing any sort of jeopardy.

A military leader maintains proper discipline, and that includes self-discipline. With the help of your senior NCOs, you'll ensure that discipline is maintained in the ranks; that is, all behavior and activity stay within the proper bounds. Discipline requires the judicious, but not necessarily continuous, application of an officer's authority. The common knowledge that you, as a strong and fair leader, will react to transgressions is normally enough to keep everything in check. Therefore, never look the other way when you see small breeches of discipline. An organization that is experiencing deteriorating discipline could quickly become dysfunctional. It won't ever come to that if you're proactive and establish the right mind-set in your branch or flight.

When you provide feedback to your people, it should be in a positive context. You should mentally rehearse the key areas you're going to cover so that you can speak with greater conviction. Emphasize the person's strengths and achievements, and articulate specific ways for him to bolster the weaker aspects of his performance. The whole experience should be candid and encouraging, and it should result in his strong commitment to maintain standards and achieve goals. The individual should walk away from the session fully convinced that you understand and appreciate his many contributions to the mission, and he should be motivated to do his very best so that he won't disappoint you, the leader he respects the most.

Expressing disappointment with an individual's performance should only be done in a private setting. Whenever you have to counsel or reprimand someone, set things up so that the individual can recover his dignity and pride in the long run. You're endeavoring to correct behavior, not to destroy the individual. If the situation gets elevated to the commander, try to influence his decision regarding the type of non-judicial punishment to be administered. Various actions the commander takes could have unintended side effects that prevent a person from reenlisting. Often times, an immature but talented troop can be given the opportunity to recover from his mistake. If he learned from the experience, he should end up being a much better airman.

If you don't like a newly assigned airman at first sight, check yourself for bias or prejudice. Then review his personnel records to learn more about him. Judge the person's past duty performance and achievements, not some stereotypical image. The presumed "geek" who is fixing your desktop computer may turn out to be an aggressive "kick-butt" warrior during a future deployment. And a muscle-bound gorilla type may turn out to be one of the most intellectual and sensitive people on your team. Yes, all people have their strong points and their weak points, but that's OK because the effective leader makes the whole team greater than the sum of its individual members.

As a company grade officer, your office administration activity will usually be done in the self-help mode; after all, you've been provided with the right information technology tools. If you're lucky enough to have an office manager (aka secretary) working for you, be sensitive to the fact that some people will resent that person "wearing your rank" while following up on overdue "suspenses." Take heed if the more experienced and senior members of the staff hint that your management assistant or office automation specialist seems to have delusions of grandeur. That may be an accurate observation or it may just be resentment; in any case, it's something to keep an eye on and to gently influence if necessary.

You probably won't have a chief working for you early on in your career, but you'll frequently interact with them. Chiefs offer their great wisdom and sage advice, and you can consider any interaction with a chief to be a gratis learning experience. Don't ever abdicate your authority and responsibility to a chief; you're the one who leads your team. But you'll certainly want to take a chief's input into account as you give orders. If you routinely involve a chief in multiple small tasks, you'll soon lose his support as he's drawn away to tackle much bigger challenges for somebody else. What's wonderful about chiefs is that if the day ever comes that you cause a minor train wreck, they'll help you pick up the pieces and they'll be discrete about it.

Your superintendent is a cut above other personnel working for you, and you'll have a somewhat unique and trusted relationship with that individual. If you understand the superintendent's role and empower him to do his job, you'll soon have your right-hand man. And you'll quickly discover that you don't have to get deep into every activity or situation because the superintendent will ensure that your people tend to the details.

The officer and the superintendent keep each other informed of internal and external activity; that keeps them both completely abreast of what's going on and ensures the continuity of operations.

If you do have senior NCOs working for you, understand that they're there to help you and everyone else achieve goals. The senior NCOs lead the smaller teams of enlisted people that you don't continually interact with. They also help you develop expertise in your specialty and serve as your coach as you interface with the more junior enlisted personnel. Plus, senior NCOs now fill numerous roles that were formerly held by officers only: safety officer, security officer, etc. A senior NCO knows that it's his duty and honor to share his wealth of experience with the company grade officers. And on those rare occasions when things go wrong because you turned a deaf ear to sound advice, he'll kindly hold back on saying, "I told you so."

You're at the helm of your branch or flight. However, you've got to trust your senior NCOs. Don't resent it when they're smarter than you in a specific situation; instead, let them know that you appreciate their experience and knowledge. Consider the brigadier general who opened a refrigerator in a break room while he was touring a squadron. The only item in that refrigerator was a very old food container. The general took out the plastic container and was about to open it when a master sergeant said in a strong but respectful voice, "General, you really don't want to do that." Needless to say, the general understood, and he did not resent the good advice.

Establish a strong professional relationship with all the NCOs on your team. You've got to win their hearts and minds, and the NCOs have got to share your vision of the future in terms of goals and success. The smart young officer may know exactly what has to be done but the NCOs are the experts who know how to actually get the job done. Therefore, think twice before you start telling a highly experienced NCO how to do his job. Keep the communications channels open; it's absolutely critical to establishing their loyalty. Also, even though it would be very comfortable to have everyone agree with everything you say, don't do anything that would cause your normally candid NCOs to join the ranks of common "yes-men."

You're running the show, but you and your troops are all in it together. The more senior troops might occasionally provide you with informal feedback in private. For example, a senior NCO might respectfully say, "L-T, good call on delaying base-wide implementation of that new system until our software ace returns from deployment next month." Or you might hear, "Boss, our loaders got all those F-16s armed just barely on time for the exercise launch; if you would have let us tailor the shift schedule a bit, we'd have had more troops on the flight line at just the right time." If you accidently overhear comments about your leadership, positive or negative, don't let on that you heard. Just keep that valuable input in mind as you lead the charge.

If you outsource a function, you might have contractors mixed in with your airmen. Remember, your lowest ranking enlisted troop outranks any contractor. Also, ensure that the contractors know you'll cry foul if they start recruiting your blue-suiters, or even you. In fact, some business developers (sly salesmen) might hint at keeping a position open for you in their firm if you'll strongly advocate their products or services to your boss. On the other hand, many defense contractors are military veterans who are very sensitive to the setting they find themselves in. If a contractor appears to be more focused on your unit's mission than his firm's profit, show you appreciate his support and treat him as a member of your team.

Your airmen certainly have the right to take a thorny issue directly to the inspector general's office or to the Equal Opportunity and Treatment office. However, they should understand that you prefer to resolve issues in house where possible, rather than immediately dragging the issues to outside agencies. That said, if you get first shot at fixing a racial issue or addressing a sexual harassment complaint, make sure that you're very firm and decisive; otherwise, the situation will fester and outside agencies will become involved. It's smart to bring the first sergeant into the picture as your consultant when you work those kinds of issues, even if that's done behind the scenes.

Know and take care of your people; they can't focus on the mission if their basic needs aren't being met or if their personal lives are in turmoil. You need to have a reasonable degree of sensitivity and empathy, and you need to be objective to address what may be a very difficult and emotional situation for the individual. Beyond that, you have to be familiar with the agencies that can help your people when they need it. The first sergeant will know the full range of services available to help your people. But don't simply throw these situations onto the nearest first sergeant; that approach is nothing more than a drive-by tactic. The proper approach is for you or one of your senior NCOs to partner with the first sergeant as he helps your troop deal with his tough personal challenge.

Company grade officers remain generally aware of what's going on in the higher levels of bureaucracy, but there's no need to generate an anxiety epidemic. You want to avoid taking your airmen on a psychological roller-coaster ride. Don't continually inform them about what could be perceived as turmoil at the Air Staff or the Joint Staff in the Pentagon. Perishable information of that nature would just distract them from their duties and could diminish their faith in the Air Force leadership. The ultimate decisions on various service-wide issues or policies can be a very long time in coming; they're likely to go through many iterations of staffing before being published in a final version and disseminated to the field.

Highlight the lighter and brighter side of military life where possible. Military duty shouldn't be pure drudgery. The Air Force isn't Disneyland but it's still OK to have fun doing the job. Some shared humor at the right time can lighten up the atmosphere and get the team to bond tighter. So a joke in good taste or a wisecrack from one of the troops shouldn't necessarily be looked upon as disruptive activity. Just make sure that no one is humiliated or embarrassed and that enthusiasm for the mission is not diminished by some cynical quip.

Take the glory off of yourself and put it on the sharp people who really got the job done. Be sure your praise is on target, giving it exactly when and where it's due. Give praise in proportion to the magnitude of the achievement and the quality of performance. Routine actions or satisfactory performance don't merit huge praise; sometimes a "well done" will do nicely. Don't succumb to or be perceived as exercising favoritism; your team has room for more than just one hero. Gently solicit letters of appreciation from entities that have been extremely well served by individuals on your team. Take advantage of visits from your commander or VIPs; they might be willing to "coin" a few of your super achievers.

Airmen also need to receive actual medals for their strong dedication and superior performance; that's partly because medals are a factor in the promotion selection process. But be careful about initiating medals in the middle of a person's tour of duty; achievements can only be recognized one time. Giving a medal for a single achievement at the mid-tour point might deprive the individual of a higher level medal at the end of his tour. Also, the magnitude and impact of an individual's achievements are the biggest determining factor for the type of medal the airman receives, no matter what his rank may be. You'll see this play out at Commander's Call.

Be a vigorous proponent of promotion for your people. Encourage them to study for promotion, and allow them time to cram a bit just prior to testing. When promotion results come out, see if the commander will let you be the one to notify your guy or gal that they've been selected for higher rank. Facilitate a classy promotion ceremony of the right proportion; this is particularly important for movement up into and through the senior NCO ranks. Hand-write a personal congratulatory note on deluxe stationary; it will be treated as a cherished keepsake. In some instances, you may even decide to present an inexpensive but clever gift for the individual to cherish as a memento of the occasion. All this wonderful activity is not disruptive; it's essential!

As a young officer, you'll have to make a conscious effort to earn the trust and respect of your team. Plus, you'll have to maintain your credibility, something that's easy to damage and hard to restore. Needless to say, the troops will dutifully render respect and salute an officer's rank, but they don't automatically respect the person wearing it. You'll know your people hold you in high esteem and care a lot about you if they tell you to duck when a "flaming arrow" is inbound towards you. However, if they don't alert you to "incoming," then you probably ought to assess the status of your relationships; perhaps some improvement could be made.

The axiom, "Nice guys finish last" is a bit unfair. Take the generals, for example; most of them are nice guys. But there's a distinct difference between being a successful nice guy and being a nice guy who is successful; you want to be the latter. As an officer, you really shouldn't be mean or intimidating by nature. However, you've got to be a tough leader in terms of moral and physical strength, and in your determination to complete the mission. In the end, your fellow airmen will respect and admire you. With that as a foundation, you'll form excellent professional relationships, and maybe even a few lifelong friendships.

Chapter 6
PRACTICAL MANAGEMENT

Young Air Force officers will find management to be an exciting activity that's replete with challenges. To succeed as a manager, you'll identify the critical path to mission success and stay mainly focused on that. You'll often be exercising top-level oversight and control over the many resources under your purview, but that doesn't imply superficial management. In fact, you'll often walk amongst your people as they make their magic happen. You'll soon discover that, with the rarest of exceptions, everyone on your team is smart, hard-working, and dedicated. That's a golden resource your civilian counterparts can never count on having. Here are some recommendations that may prove useful as you step into the world of military management.

Align your team's goals with those set by your commander. Express them in concrete, objective terms such as percentages of standards, frequency of events, etc. Goals should be jointly established by all parties involved, not arbitrarily set. Of course, you're going to set the bar high, but make goals realistic in terms of achievability and acceptability; for example, a 98 percent system availability rate may be totally unacceptable, but a 100 percent availability rate may be unrealistic and unreasonably high. Goals need to be conspicuously displayed so that everyone stays synchronized and moving in the right direction. Progress in achieving those goals needs to be jointly reviewed on at least a monthly basis.

Excellence does not necessarily imply perfection. Perfection is somewhat of a luxury in today's "do-more-with-less" culture. In some instances, satisfactory results are plenty good enough; that is, when your product or service is well within specifications. Of course, there are some specific functions or processes in which perfection is an absolute imperative; examples are: adherence to safety procedures, management of nuclear weapons, control of cryptographic material, etc. Be sure to share your conclusions on this subject with your boss so that his expectations are properly set.

Change happens at such a fast pace that it's difficult to map out and control passage into the future. Even so, you can't just react to change; you've got to anticipate it so that you can plan new processes and tailor organizational structures. This requires you to keep an eye on the horizon and to listen carefully when your boss explains the developments occurring in the big picture. Remember to expect some resistance to change; it can't be rammed down people's throats. Explaining what's driving the change, agreeing on a change strategy, and predicting the resulting benefits may be enough to persuade your people to buy into their own imminent future.

There's a shred of truth to the old cliché that says officers are promoted to their next level of incompetence. Junior officers are assigned to new positions based on their need for experience. No worries for you though; an officer who is a quick study can gain competency through total immersion in branch or flight activities. That's kind of like being thrown into rough seas in a "sink-or-swim" scenario, except that you've got great people to keep you buoyed up. As you get "spun-up" in your new duties, keep in mind that you can only blame your predecessor for existing problems during your first six months on the job; after the six-month point, you're to blame for anything that's still broken, and you get the glory for everything that's working right.

Alas, multitasking has become a way of life for managers; you're given multiple tasks and you're multitasking people who work for you. To deal with all that simultaneous activity, you'll need a "heads-up display" (HUD) that shows the progress of each function or project and the level of available resources. A HUD can be easily created as a web-based system that allows your key people to perform checks or updates at any time from anywhere. Whenever your team members meet with you to view the HUD, they'll all see a graphic presentation of progress and areas needing attention. That goes a long way toward establishing accountability, peer pressure, and pride.

Some activities under your purview don't require constant monitoring and control. Determine which processes are most critical to a particular project or program; then periodically check those key indicators in the form of metrics to ensure the project or program is on track and progressing as planned. That targeted type of monitoring, coupled with occasional verbal reports from your people, helps ensure you don't get bogged down in micromanagement and lose sight of the bigger picture. Plus, it allows you to embrace a broader range of activities.

If you try to do everything yourself, you'll get so wrapped around the axle that you'll lose your bearings and, in effect, leave your team without a leader. Delegate at least to the point where you don't find yourself routinely working issues way down in the weeds. You should also judiciously delegate selected functions to the right people in order to provide them with challenges that result in their professional growth. Establish accountability for on-time results when you delegate, and do the same when you assign projects or tasks. When you present the results to the boss, be sure that all the credit and praise goes to the person who produced the results.

Don't be a "spring-butt" junior officer who volunteers his team to do anything and everything just so he can gain more laurels for himself. Ask yourself a few questions first: What's the return on investment for my organization and troops? Is it a challenge my people would enjoy tackling? How will they view it from an equity standpoint—our flight versus other less tasked flights? Is my boss aware that I'm committing the unit's resources to a new initiative? There are indeed various occasions where you and your team should cheerfully step up to the plate and do something extra for the greater good of the organization or the community; just look carefully before you leap.

Where possible, prioritize and pace mission activity so that it remains fairly level, rather than cycling through huge peaks and lulls. Take into account forthcoming absences due to deployments, school, and leaves so that you don't get caught short on personnel. Preannounce big events where possible so that your people can schedule their leave plans accordingly; gracefully get them to reschedule if their absence could negatively impact the mission. Watch out for too many people postponing their Air Expeditionary Force deployment windows; your manpower could become depleted if all the make-up deployments get bunched together.

Pick the right time to prepare your branch or flight for a unit inspection. Don't put that on the team as an extra burden until you get close to the actual event, perhaps four months out. Meanwhile, your direction and guidance should keep operations generally in line with current Air Force policy and instructions. Keep tabs on what inspectors are checking in units similar to yours and make a list of those items. When the time is right, create an individually tailored checklist for each of your work centers to use as a supplement to self-inspection guides while they prepare for the inspection. Also, don't push your troops to earn an "outstanding" rating, but do hold them accountable to achieve a rating of "excellent."

There are various ways to turn around a faltering work center. You can implement better procedures, provide targeted training, reconfigure the layout, refurbish the facility, or replace the leader. If the work center is simply task-saturated, prioritize tasks so that only the legitimate and critical ones are dealt with, leaving the rest to be handled if and when time permits. If need be, set yourself up as the gatekeeper for the tasking of that work center, rather than allowing sundry jobs to flow into the work center through the back door. It would be smart to involve your people in analyzing the management problem and developing a get-well plan; it may even be beneficial to organize an "off-site" meeting to conduct this diagnostic activity.

Very few projects at the field unit level require formal program management. Oversee your project, but also assign one of your more seasoned NCOs to "ramrod" the project. Be leery of proposed projects that have too many phases over too long a period of time; such projects might not get completed during your tenure or might even be overcome by events. Planning and foresight are critical in this era of just-in-time logistics. It's absolutely imperative that you have the required resources in place at the right time; otherwise, your project could lose momentum or be delayed. The danger with delays is that it's difficult to reorganize the precious human resources needed to revive a dormant project.

Manpower engineers do not administer any anesthetic when they perform surgery, and manpower cuts can be extremely painful. In this era of diminishing resources, the manpower gurus will constantly force you to re-justify why you need your airmen. Maintain a soft-copy file of all position descriptions, including text that justifies why each manpower position is needed and explains what part of the mission would "break" if the position were to remain unfilled or be eliminated. That data will have you spring-loaded for the inevitable manpower surveys and zero-base manpower studies.

Seek out topnotch personnel for your branch or flight, rather than waiting for the personnel system to flow a "warm body" to your team. Even though the assignment system is semi-automated, a by-name request for a sharp airman is still worth the effort. Have the airman simultaneously request assignment to your team, thereby making the process a push-pull effort. Sometimes you'll be able to recruit a recently promoted individual from another organization if he's in search of a bigger job. Be sure to work that action through the individual's unit commander; dirty deals worked through the back door generate resentment and often backfire.

Serious personnel problems must be dealt with head-on. Whether it's early in your career or much later on, you may encounter a person in your unit who has a severe, maybe even chronic, behavioral problem. You could hide the problem, but that puts the mission at risk, particularly in terms of safety and security. Or you could eject the person; that's a huge administrative undertaking and leaves a hard-to-fill vacuum. The right thing to do is to invest the considerable time and energy it takes to help the individual help himself, thereby restoring the person's dignity and keeping him on the job. However, if the person resents the help and fails to "normalize," you must quickly remove him, without passing the problem on to someone else.

Be careful when releasing your people to participate in some endeavor that's supported by a matrix organization. Call for a "time-out" if you feel outsiders are gutting your team to seize human resources for their own project or program. Make sure your boss is aware that you have some of your people committed to activity that's not in your immediate domain. If he's made aware early on, he'll be in a better position to intercede on your behalf if it becomes necessary. The same applies to equity; if the boss isn't aware of tasking placed on you by outside entities, he'll just keep flowing more tasking to you rather than other branches that may be less burdened.

Establish a good rapport with the unit resource manager. The R-M will look out for your interests and be your advocate to the boss if you make realistic and well-justified input to the budget planning process. Actually, it's truly amazing to see how much the R-M can influence senior decision makers, particularly as they seize control of the funding flow in the later part of the fiscal year. You may find all the frantic activity at the beginning and end of every fiscal year to be a bit unnerving; however, you've got to get into the game in order to have any chance of winning the funds you need.

When a much needed resource magically appears, accept a senior NCO's explanation of how the badly needed item suddenly materialized. You might even hear the sincere words, "Boss, you really don't want to know." Hopefully, your people adhered to the spirit of the law as they violated the letter of the law. But even if they did violate an instruction, their intent may override the transgression as long as there were no associated safety issues and no one else's mission capability was diminished. You may, however, have to feign a mild public scolding of the senior NCO, as you wink at him.

There will be the odd time when it's smart for you to personally fund purchases of small items needed for a special event or ceremony. For example, your troops may want to make a small cosmetic improvement to the work center or provide a special going away gift to a departing airman. The unit's local purchase credit card can't be used for anything and everything; sometimes it's better to cheerfully chip in five or ten dollars so a quick purchase can be made downtown. By the way, there's really no need to tell your spouse about those occasional out-of-pocket expenditures.

Today's CGO has got to learn how to do more with less. One strategy is to "automate" functions or services through the use of web-based technology. However, don't let some slick software engineer build you a unique system that only he can maintain. That system will falter and disintegrate soon after he's reassigned. It's far better to expedite automation via Air Force approved commercial off-the-shelf software (aka enterprise software). Also, be sure to consolidate and incorporate appropriate functions from costly legacy systems that you absolutely must abandon once the new system is operational. Implement your new system in phases by building on incremental successes rather than struggling with a big-bang approach.

Don't get bogged down by the administrative aspects of your office. Strive to achieve a paperless office—a holy grail. If a mundane document sits in your in-basket for more than a week, place it in the lower left drawer of your desk; then consider discarding the document once it ferments in there for a month. Hold soft copies of documents in well-organized computer files and properly marked computer disks. Avoid making hard copies of classified documents; instead, use the data repository available on the classified network. Invest the time needed to properly organize your e-mail service; this will save you time in the long run, and preclude lots of frustration.

Install specially authorized government owned productivity software on your home computer so that you can work on documents and briefings without going into the office on weekends. Not only does this keep you closer to your family, it will also save you travel time; plus, you won't get caught up in frivolous dialogue with the few other folks who happen to be in the building. Where possible, get software installed on your home

PC that allows you to check official e-mail and access the Air Force Portal website from home. Again, this will enable you to extend your office hours without actually being in the office.

If you're standing in for your boss at a meeting, try to avoid committing your organization to a new project or activity. If called upon to make a commitment, simply say that the request or idea certainly seems to have merit, but you'll have to interact with your boss to see if resources are available to deal with expanded mission activity. Then do some quick checking for any history on this new situation and estimate the resources needed to support it. Now that you're armed with relevant data, explain everything to your boss in a calm and objective manner, and then provide him with your smart recommendation.

The white glove inspection is a long-abandoned ritual. Even so, a work center's appearance greatly influences the quality of work produced there. Here are some eyesores that you can zero in on: faded paint, shabby partitions, broken furniture, threadbare carpet, missing fluorescent tubes, makeshift signage, and general clutter. When replacing carpet, always opt for carpet tiles rather than huge expanses of carpeting; then keep several cases of spare tiles stowed away. Also, don't use bargain basement solutions to coat garage and hangar floors. Be aware that civil engineers can't take on spontaneous "flip-this-work-center" projects; any renovation effort must combine self-help enhancements (to start) with fully planned and funded upgrades.

If a new facility is created or undergoes a complete renovation, you might want to organize a ribbon-cutting ceremony to open or restart the facility. A short speech by you at the start of the ceremony would bring it all into focus and create an opportunity to recognize the major players. Presentation of an achievement medal to the principal player, with Public Affairs present, would also be an appropriate element of the ceremony. Such an event establishes an aura of prestige and instills pride in those who are going to operate the facility. Everyone involved will be delighted with the ceremony, including the civil engineer, the contracting officer, and your commander.

Emphasize and publicize the ongoing positive activity and achievements of your branch or flight. Objectively deal with the negative factors behind the scenes, and downplay them. Many of those negative issues can be worked after the fact. If your hot rod is winning the quarter-mile race, why slow down to advertise and address the fact that the left fender is scratched and the engine is a little low on oil. You can't permanently ignore those issues, but you should not waste time and energy focusing on them while the race is on. Streak to the finish line in style!

Military business isn't always blissful. You'll occasionally get involved in consternation and contention; however, you have to pick your fights. Think before engaging: is the issue a big deal and is the fight winnable? Sometimes you're sure you could win the battle but there's nothing really big at stake and the victory isn't worth the resentment that would follow. Other times, the battle might not be winnable because of the opponent's political clout. Then again, there may be times when it's absolutely imperative that you "take it to the mat," such as a situation where one of your troops was seriously wronged. In any event, if you pick and choose your battles, you'll win a greater percentage of them and you'll maintain a bigger population of allies.

Be a student of politics but don't get tangled up in political turmoil. Politics are an element of doing business in any organization; fortunately for you, it's a small element of the Air Force culture and it's pretty much restricted to the upper ranks. So just be sensitive to your boss's position and be loyal to him. By the same token, continue to observe the political goings-on and analyze events so that you'll develop a reasonable degree of political savvy in the long run. You also need to be aware of the good old boy/gal network and how it can sometimes control events, often in your favor. The good news is that this special type of networking doesn't dominate Air Force business, and when such activity takes place, it's usually beneficial in the grand scheme of things.

You'll purge your desktop computer as you transfer out to your next assignment, so you need to create a continuity folder for your successor. Go ahead and scribe a few important notes, but don't spend a lot of time creating literary content for the folder. Instead, toss these readily available items into the folder: the mission statement, your flight's goals, your position description, organizational charts, personnel listings, relevant policy letters, a copy of the current budget statement, a list of telephone and e-mail contacts, a list of useful military internet URLs, and various on-hand documents that succinctly portray the main systems, programs and projects.

Chapter 7
EFFECTIVE COMMUNICATIONS

Air Force officers spend what seems to be an inordinate amount of time communicating in various modes. You'll frequently write documents, prepare graphics, and present briefings. In the early stages of your career, most of that activity is done by you rather than for you. The good news is that you'll have a lot of high-tech tools at your disposal. In fact, you're in the Information Age where some would argue that the keyboard is mightier than the sword, particularly the cadre engaged in information warfare. At any rate, all successful officers are effective and efficient communicators.

Military writing is an acquired skill that gets honed by practicing the trade. The achievements of your people are portrayed in performance reports and award submissions; learn to write them extremely well, using an active style. That means making powerful statements that have a high degree of objectivity, with statistical data imbedded where possible. Remember, board members reviewing promotion folders have precious little time to read each document; so articulate a great feat at the beginning of the document to grab the reader's attention, and save a couple of high impact achievements for the end of the product where they'll be more conspicuous.

Learn to write telegraphically. This special technique is actually an art form, and it's critical for bullet background papers, point papers, performance reports, promotion recommendations, award packages, and other documents. Crafting documents in this high-impact style involves creative phrase structure, clever punctuation, powerful words, and fresh phrases (as opposed to clichés). Common acronyms are also used to compress the text and make it even more hard-hitting. However, when striving for brevity, don't go so far as to make the text too stilted or cryptic.

In the case of performance reports and award packages, it's alright to push the envelope when expressing the magnitude of achievements, but it's necessary to stay within the bounds of truth and credibility. Always express achievements in terms of the big picture, and relate them to aviation and airpower. That's because you're in the <u>Air</u> Force, with rated (flying) officers dominating the leadership. Selection board members might not care much about the new X-band satellite communications link that your technicians activated to reach an overseas location. But they sure would take notice of something like this, "Activated huge data pipe for remote control of Predator Ops in GWOT hot spot—target kills up 40 percent."

Don't ask your people to write their own performance reports or awards. But do get them to give you carefully prepared notes about their performance and achievements. There are two reasons why you should get input from the people you are rating. First, your troops might articulate a significant achievement that you initially didn't recall. Second, your precious time is best spent polishing and inserting gems into the reports, rather than mining for those gems. Even though your people provide you with substantial and valid input, your creative touch will be evident in the final version of the products. In other words, they give you the basic car and then you chop, cut and rebuild to create a dream performance report or award package.

Pay your dues to your airmen as you leave for a new PCS assignment. Write appropriate award and decoration packages on your key people and give the drafts to your successor. Your successor can hardly be expected to work up rock-solid award nomination packages soon after his arrival. Even though personnel files may contain information about your airmen's achievements, it would be tough for your successor to get all their past deeds into focus based on fragments of history. Also, pass your people copies of the drafts behind the scenes so that they'll know you thought enough of them to initiate their award submissions before you blasted off to your next duty assignment.

Always put forward a maximum effort on award citations even if you have to do some of that work on the kitchen table at home. Those citations will be read aloud in a formal ceremony, often with an airman's family members present. That's a great opportunity for everyone to develop an appreciation for the airman's achievements, and the overall mission. The citations are also placed in the promotion folders of both officers and enlisted personnel; therefore, they're a significant factor in determining who is selected for promotion. A spin-off benefit of your literary endeavors is that your seniors review those citations during the award approval process; thus, they become even more aware of the great work being done under your leadership.

Keep a few of the best bullet background papers and talking papers that you've read. Save them as soft copies on your computer so you can use them as templates for a "plug and play" writing experience. That way, you'll avoid having to "reinvent the wheel" each time your boss calls for a product with very little lead time. If your boss states that a bullet background paper is needed by close of business two days from now and you finish it a day early, hold off on presenting the paper to him until the day it's due. That gives you a chance to look at it with fresh eyes the next morning, at which time you'll surely groom the paper a bit so you can present a sterling product to the boss.

When preparing correspondence, put yourself in the reader's shoes and assess your tone from his perspective in order to ensure that your words aren't inadvertently rude or harsh; this is especially important if the reader is senior to you. For example, if your letter or e-mail sternly demands something from another organization, you may end up being told that you will indeed get what you're entitled to, but only after going through a long series of bureaucratic wickets. Had you made the request in a more civil manner, the reader may have been inclined to help you out by cutting the bureaucratic wickets down to just a few, or even none.

You'll review and edit many draft documents. Use a green or blue pen when you edit the hard-copy text that your people draft for you. Red pens aggravate people on a subconscious level because that's what their stern schoolteachers used for grading tests and papers. Also, don't waste time converting someone else's draft to your personal writing style if the message is already clearly stated. Finally, when the Air Force Academy's professional writing "road show" comes to your base, make sure that you and your key people attend that micro course. The Academy's English professors will quickly impart many valuable writing tricks and techniques.

Whenever possible, delay sending your initial version of e-mails and letters to persons of significantly higher rank until the next morning, after you've had a chance to check your draft with fresh eyes and to take into account recent developments. You'll inevitably edit your correspondence and make the text clearer; you may even refine the tone of the communication. There's no point in sending a feverishly written e-mail that's dripping with emotion, only to learn that it was overcome by events not long after being sent. And trying to call an e-mail back is an exercise in futility; once you send it, consider it to have been read.

The most important thing about an e-mail or message is the address—who is talking to whom and who is courtesy-copied or "info'd" in the communication. In other words, who are the players in this issue and who is aware of it? Also, don't have a prematurely violent reaction to a sour e-mail; the way an issue is hastily expressed often looks worse in the e-mail than it actually is. Be careful with the use of all capital letters in words and phrases; the receiver may interpret your emphasis as anger or rage. The occasional smiley face :>) is very useful to defuse a situation or to convey a positive or cheerful attitude about a particularly challenging situation. Think fast if your boss sends you the opposite. :>(

If your boss provides you a cell phone or BlackBerry, monitor it continuously after regular business hours. That way, your boss will sense that you're at his side 24/7, ready to help out in any situation. Don't courtesy-copy your boss on too many e-mails. And give your boss a heads-up if you're going to blind-copy him on a contentious e-mail going to another organization. If you don't, you may find yourself in an awkward situation when the boss responds to your e-mail using the "reply all" function. Plus, the higher the rank of the person you're e-mailing, the shorter your e-mail should be. There are even a few cantankerous flag officers who refuse to read e-mails longer than five lines, treating them as though they were spam.

Speak to others with confidence, conviction, and enthusiasm. Use a strong voice but not overly loud, and don't broadcast at an octave far below your natural voice in order to appear ultra macho. A struggling tenor will most certainly ruin the opera. There are even a few tough lady officers who fall into that trap. If you're addressing a critical issue, be reasonably intense and show a bit of fire in your eyes. It's OK to be openly passionate about an issue, just don't get too emotional. Rather than act gruff and intimidating, be sure to naturally smile at the appropriate times as you're interacting with people. The occasional smile indicates that you have great self-confidence and that you're approachable.

Maintain eye contact when communicating with people; one's eyes convey sincerity and reinforce what's being said. They also reveal the receiver's reaction to what he has just heard. Therefore, if you're wearing sunglasses while interacting with a senior officer, take them off if there is no strong sun shining directly in your eyes. Don't ever wear mirror sunglasses; no one likes conversing with people who wear that type of glasses. Perhaps it has something to do with the stereotype of the "evil" prison guard depicted in movies, such as the classic film *Cool Hand Luke*.

Slang and colloquialisms should be used sparingly, not as a natural and routine way of expressing oneself. You're not talking to your "buds" on campus or your "bros" in the hood. "That's pretty cool, dude" is hardly the same as an officer saying, "Awesome product, Sergeant Jones." The same holds true for exaggerated country-boy talk; a quaint vernacular might amuse people but it will probably inhibit communications. Granted, you'll occasionally hear a seasoned colonel or chief portray himself as the poor old country boy who has a good horse-sense solution to a perplexing problem—"If y'all are interested."

Volunteer to read award citations at ceremonies. It's a great way to become accustomed to speaking in front of large audiences. Print out a black and white copy rather than read the beige certificate in poor light. Practice out loud and heavily mark punctuation on the paper to ensure that the narrative will read clearly and smoothly. Practice reading the text several times, but not so many times that your mind would start to wander while reading the citation during the actual ceremony. It's an Air Force citation, so your voice should sound serious and official but not overly dramatic. In the absence of a microphone, project your voice but not to the point of straining it.

You'll occasionally have to create briefings. Limit the briefing content to just a few main points that are organized in a logical sequence so they build upon each other. Use a powerful statement or anecdote to introduce your main theme. Avoid verbatim briefing scripts unless absolutely necessary; instead, use groups of bullet phrases in large print to guide a more extemporaneous and enthusiastic presentation. Rehearse the whole briefing, preferably in the room where you'll give your presentation. Place a beverage, preferably water, at the podium just before the briefing starts. Finally, deliver your briefing in a confident manner that's not too intense.

The slides you create for briefings shouldn't be wordy or cluttered, but they must convey the message, even without the associated briefing text. Be sure to clearly spell out the essentials of the concept and the expected end result. A picture is worth a thousand words, so it's smart to include a couple of photos or drawings. Don't load up your slides with distracting bells, whistles and special effects; they may cause attendees to wonder if you and your people have too much free time on your hands. While selecting font sizes, keep in mind that the briefing slides are not supposed to be an eye test for senior military officers.

Whenever you're in proximity of voice and video teleconference systems, assume that microphones and cameras are always activated and that participants can hear and see you all the time. While that may seem paranoid, careless people inevitably say or do something embarrassing before their conferencing equipment is actually muted or the cameras are turned off. Consider your attire for video teleconferences; you might not want to appear in your pristine service dress uniform when participants on the other end of the teleconference are dressed for combat. If available, make sure that the dial-up telephone conferencing capability is tested and ready as a backup to the video connection.

Always keep in mind that some members of the press may tend to quote you out of context in order to spice up the news, which they themselves are sometimes creating. Refer reporters to the Public Affairs office, or at least interact with the press under the auspices of the Public Affairs Officer. That aside, there are members of the press who boldly go in harm's way along with the troops. Members of the press have learned to respect Operations Security, particularly since scores of them have been killed in Iraq. Even so, be extra careful about what you reveal to them; you don't want plans for your unit's next mission to inadvertently end up on the next CNN or Fox News broadcast.

Use the Public Affairs office to highlight the achievements and success of your people. That may require you to partner with the Public Affairs staff and write a rough draft newspaper article for them, or at least provide extensive details. If they're filming you and/or your airmen, personally check to be sure that those in the spotlight are in compliance with dress and appearance standards, including weight standards. If security considerations allow it, always keep a digital camera close at hand to capture important events "on film." The few remaining base photographers are no longer at everyone's beck and call, particularly since they're frequently deployed to tactical settings.

Be careful when spontaneously labeling facilities or capabilities. Two examples are, calling the flag officer's "Airborne Rest and Conference Cabin" an aircraft "Comfort Capsule," and calling a wing commander's new conference room "The boss's Taj Mahal." Such labels carry unexpected connotations (in this case extravagance and waste). That's just what disgruntled dime-droppers are looking for. Inadvertently creating such misperceptions can put senior leaders in a bad light and can generate serious allegations.

Avoid hogging the show when a high-ranking officer visits. A flag officer or Special Executive Service civilian will only open up their mind to absorb one or two important things that you say; everything else is just lots of pleasant chatting. But do some homework ahead of time so that you're primed to succinctly answer any questions the Distinguished Visitor may pose. You can add a bit of highly relevant information to your response, as long as it doesn't upstage or embarrass your boss. When accompanying a D-V on a tour of your work centers, briefly mention the nature of the work center's activity and any recently earned awards; then gracefully hand the D-V off to the NCO in charge. It's his turn to shine.

You have lots of important information to convey, but sometimes you'll have to consciously switch to the receive mode so you can really hear what your people are saying. Also, it's rather unfair for an officer to take advantage of captive audiences. Your respectful airmen don't really need to hear about all the wonderful things going on in your privileged officer life, or even your personal problems. However, you need to hear about the challenges they face and the activities going on in their lives. Your airmen look up to you, so, the empathy, encouragement and approval you give them will be highly beneficial and greatly appreciated.

Chapter 8
BULLETPROOF CONDUCT

As an Air Force officer, your superior integrity and demeanor are what make you stand out in a crowd. People know you can always be counted on to do the right thing, even if it's just for the sake of doing the right thing. Because perceptions count, you'll even find yourself taking steps to ensure that no one could possibly perceive your conduct as being anything less than honorable. Thirty or forty years ago, some airmen joined in on outrageous behavior; some looked the other way as it went on, and others tolerated it because they felt intimidated by rank. In today's Air Force, there's total transparency and accountability, and the contemporary officer is comfortable with that.

Officers compete amongst themselves; however, good sportsmanship must prevail in all situations. If you "steal" resources from another officer's domain or take credit for some other officer's work, it will always come back to haunt you. Rest assured that the Air Force is pretty much devoid of cutthroat politics, back-stabbing, kowtowing, cheap shots and other such sinister activities that permeate corporate America. In the Air Force, you'll be able to operate with a high degree of confidence that there won't be any "fratricide" amongst the officers as they conduct their business.

A shadow of doubt on an officer's character, even if unjustified, could put him in a bad light. The mere appearance of improper conduct has essentially the same effect as actually committing the act. Picture the male lieutenant who is working with the spouse's club to organize the squadron's Christmas party. The young L-T needs to coordinate with one of the key spouses, a sergeant's very pretty wife. The L-T parks his red sports car in the driveway of the sergeant's on-base quarters twice to confer with the wife; oddly enough, the sergeant is away on duty both times. The L-T didn't really do anything wrong, but misperceptions of improper conduct are likely to morph into serious allegations.

There's always plenty of exuberance when a huge goal is achieved. That's as it should be, but an officer must ensure that manifestations of exuberance don't spin out of control. Consider the young lieutenant who turns around a historically weak maintenance branch and receives a high rating from a major command inspection team. There's a celebration party soon thereafter, during which time the euphoric L-T lowers his trousers, bends over, and pretends to moon the Inspector General. Such behavior would be cheered in a college frat house, but in this case it's likely to be deemed conduct unbecoming an officer. There could be serious ramifications, including the "red-lining" of the officer's pending promotion.

An officer who ogles the enlisted ladies and flirts with them might inadvertently light a fire that can't be put out, and he'll probably get burned. Even if he were just trying to amuse himself by "pushing the envelope," there's some chemistry that needs to be taken into account. The nineteen-year-old enlisted gal may have groomed herself to be extremely attractive (literally), and she may be totally enthralled with the captain's rank, status and lifestyle. Then the captain boldly feigns that he has a serious interest in the young lady and makes some provocative remarks—kaboom! By the way, the genders just portrayed could be swapped.

Think twice before meeting alone with a member of the opposite sex in closed-door sessions. Here are two very different scenarios; one is probably risky and the other is certainly safe. First, a very young enlisted gal wearing jogging togs unexpectedly enters your office at 1730 hours and announces that she wants to speak with you; she gives you a warm smile as she closes the office door behind her and then approaches you. On another occasion, a female senior master sergeant in uniform shows up at 1000 hours and says, "We need to talk, sir; may I close the door?" Always invite another person to join you in your office whenever you feel uneasy about meeting alone with a member of the opposite sex.

Officers stay true to their spouses. The spouse follows the officer as he's transferred from base to base, as did the wives of the Roman soldiers. The military spouse often minimizes her professional career in deference to her husband's career. She also acts as a pseudo aide de camp, routinely tending to a multitude of important tasks, and she's the "heavy lifter" when it's time to move the household. She also fends for herself and the family while the officer is deployed. Just those sacrifices alone merit total loyalty. Married officers should realize that intruders with amorous intentions may be more smitten with love for the officer's uniform than the person who is wearing it. Never be lured by the song of the Sirens; they'll surely wreck a happy marriage.

Travel expense claims undergo extremely close scrutiny. Don't declare an expense on a travel voucher unless you have the receipt as proof. Retain copies of orders, travel vouchers, tickets, and receipts well into your next assignment. Do at least a cursory trip report that explains the purpose of your travel, who you met with, what briefings you attended, and the outcome of the trip. If you combine leave with your government travel, make sure the government is not paying for any expenses related to the side trip back to your hometown or vacation spot. And in those instances, make sure you can demonstrate why you were the right person to have gone on the government-funded trip.

Never accept any type of gift from a contractor. Some defense contractors will innocently present you with a gift in appreciation for your collaboration in a joint endeavor. On the other hand, unscrupulous contractors may try to entrap you; they might even engrave your name and the logo of their firm on the gift. It's best to say that you appreciate the kind gesture but don't want to accept gifts of any kind. If an unsolicited gift is mailed or transported to your office, send it back via certified mail. If people saw the unsolicited gift arrive, bring someone from the office along with you when you go to the post office so word will get around that you returned the gift.

Never sell anything to an enlisted person except an automobile or a home, and in such cases you must ensure that the car or house being sold to the enlisted troop is in absolutely superb condition. In other words, everyone has to perceive that you're giving the enlisted troop the better end of the deal on the sale of your car or home. If the enlisted person feels cheated in the end, you'll be in an awkward situation and your reputation will suffer badly. It's not much different when selling personal items to a fellow officer, but if you do employ the caveat emptor approach in the sale of your flawed property, keep in mind that paybacks are hell.

Bragging about your personal financial success to the enlisted troops will probably generate resentment because many of them don't have the financial resources to dabble in the stock market or to make real estate investments. Likewise, don't work on your investment portfolio while on duty or in front of the enlisted troops. Some examples: making stock transactions on your office computer, calling your investment broker via the office phone, and so on. If an officer has enough time to conduct the business of a day trader, then it's very apparent that he hasn't been sufficiently challenged in his military job.

Be a little sensitive to others who don't possess your financial wherewithal. Don't gloat if you're lucky enough to have a new Mercedes or Lexus in the parking lot. However, be sure to praise your troop's recently acquired Mazda or Chevy, even if it's not brand new. Paying a compliment to the enlisted person certainly isn't fraternization, "Hey, Airman Smith, nice job of tricking out that Honda; sharp looking chrome rims!" Likewise, you probably don't need to flash your Rolex or Omega everywhere. "Geez, L-T, you've got a fifty thousand dollar ride and wear a five thousand dollar watch. I'm working a part-time job after duty hours just to pay the rent and keep my kid in pampers; I guess I'll always be stuck at the bottom of the food chain..."

Be humble and gracious as you take advantage of special perks. You'll have multiple opportunities to experience the finer things in life, even while performing official duties. For example, during your duty travel you might "thumb a ride" on a small executive jet that's ferrying a flag officer. You might tour a historic citadel or visit a palatial government building while escorting a distinguished visitor. As a branch chief or flight commander, you might even have your own reserved parking spot. There will ultimately be plenty of perks, none of which should be flaunted and all of which should be added to your collection of cherished memories.

Never assume that you have head-of-line privileges based on your lieutenant or captain rank. But it's appropriate to offer head-of-line privileges to a full colonel or above and to commanders. They'll sometimes turn your offer down, or you'll find they've arrived for their customer service session as a scheduled appointment. If you also happen to have such an appointment, mention it to the customer service rep as you're signing in at the desk; that will make everyone in the waiting area aware that you're not getting special treatment ahead of the other customers who have been patiently waiting for service.

As a company grade officer, you should discourage your spouse from trying to "wear" or flaunt your rank to take advantage of special officer privileges, which are relatively few at this early point in your career. But don't be taken aback by the spouse of a commander or very senior officer who wears her husband's rank in certain situations. That lady is most likely engaged in quasi official duties or some protocol activity that directly supports her husband and the unit. When a lady is so engaged, she is addressed in public as "ma'am" rather than by her first name.

Officers don't routinely commute to and from the base on motorcycles, and the general consensus is that the fewer military "bikers" there are, the better for the Air Force. However, Sunday afternoon cruising on motorcycles seems to have become a widespread practice, even amongst flag officers. So while officers may own and ride motorcycles, there still is a widespread opinion that motorcycles are very dangerous. Therefore, be aware that some of your seniors might view your routine commutes to the base via motorcycle as wrongly encouraging all the troops to join in on the risky fun.

Officers never drink alcohol to an excess in public; in fact, even just one Driving Under the Influence (DUI) or Driving While Intoxicated (DWI) incident will destroy an officer's career. If you notice that a fellow airman, no matter what the rank, has had too much to drink, make sure he has a safe ride home, even if you have to provide it yourself. If at all possible, do it without causing the person any embarrassment. Remember, some of the younger troops may be enjoying alcohol for the very first time in their lives. And if one of your airmen happens to have a serious drinking problem, reach out to help him. Pretending the problem isn't there won't make it go away, and the sooner you address it the easier it is to deal with.

There are still a few die-hard smokers out there, including officers. Smokers are the unfortunate victims of aggressive and ruthless marketing on the part of tobacco companies. Any form of tobacco use is self-destructive behavior, and both the act of using it and the result of using it will inhibit duty performance. Plus, smoking makes a person appear to be weak-willed, especially in the case of officers. Smokers should quit buying tobacco products; instead, the money should go towards something that contributes to the joy of living, such as horseback riding, sailing lessons, or even monthly payments on a new jet ski. Also, a few airmen and civilian employees still routinely step outside for a smoke break; that could be tolerable if they're productive people, but it would be unacceptable if they're just "blowing smoke" on the job.

Officers shouldn't be encumbered with heavy or multiple items as they move about. Ask for assistance if you have to carry several bulky items, or make two trips rather than be so overloaded that you're unable to return a salute. Such a breach of courtesy is a hugely awkward situation for everyone involved. Actually, one of your troops will probably approach you to kindly offer you their assistance when they notice your predicament. You should gratefully accept, but carry at least a token portion of the load so that you don't create the impression of being some sort self-designated prima donna.

You must be equally fair and impartial with all of your airmen even though you don't treat them exactly the same as individuals. And don't be receptive to undue influence from any one individual. In fact, be a little suspect of the enlisted troop who continually does favors for you, some of them falling into the realm of personal favors. There might be a price to pay later when the individual comes around asking for special treatment or reciprocal favors. How can you say no after he commandeered a brand new desk for your office, got tickets for the play your wife wants to see, and "babysat" your dog for free while you were on leave? When such a person paves the road in front of you with gold bricks, he might actually be making an investment in his own future.

If you hear sexist jokes or racial slurs, step in immediately and forcefully to terminate that activity. Not only is it totally unacceptable behavior, it can be very destructive to unit morale and esprit de corps. Plus, there's bound to be big trouble in several forms if it's perceived that you knew about such behavior and let it continue. When you intervene, the victims must be aware that you nipped it in the bud, and you need to document that fact. You can deal with it "in-house" at first, but if it persists, you'll need to get very rigorous and formal in the action you take. Make sure that your commander and first sergeant are privy to all actions, particularly if an outside agency will be brought into the picture.

The Air Force is one of America's biggest and best melting pots. Any military officer who is uncomfortable working with or for another officer who happens to be a minority group member really needs to get help from a counselor. This would also include a minority group member that may not want to serve with or under another minority group member, and also for anyone who doesn't want to work for a lady officer. If the officer can't overcome his prejudice, then it's probably best that he hang up his uniform and vector off to some dark corner of society where such behavior is condoned, and there may not even be any such places left.

Do not continually address your airmen by their first name; normally use the military title that they've earned. It's perfectly acceptable to address your airmen by their first name in special circumstance such as their birthday, to express congratulations, or when expressing sympathy in a grief situation. It's never appropriate for an enlisted troop to address an officer by his first name—not even on the ball field. In the event that situation occurs, two things have to happen. First, quickly correct the troop no matter how awkward it feels. Second, figure out why the troop felt free to take such a liberty, and then make adjustments on your part to ensure that it doesn't happen again, especially within earshot of your boss.

Think carefully before speaking during conferences and meetings. Here's one scenario: Conference attendees pose a longstanding problem to their flag officer host. A captain from the general's staff has a solution in his hip pocket. The captain excitedly blurts out, "We already came up with a great solution to that problem over a week ago." Unfortunately, he forgot that the general is totally unaware of his innovative solution. Now the general looks clueless about what his staff is doing as they run amuck. The captain should have either pulled the general's chief of staff aside and mentioned the solution, or provided it later as a smart response to a formal tasking.

An officer never talks behind anyone's back unless he's saying something good about them. If you hear gossip, find a subtle way to communicate that it's inappropriate; such as, "Come on, folks, let's just roll up our sleeves and tackle the rest of this report that's due today." Also, avoid complaining to your seniors about the faltering performance of one of your troops, unless you are in dire need of some advice. On the other hand, you may have a success story for the boss if your leadership converts a "problem child" into a strong performer. In fact, you might even brag about a particular person to your superiors if you're advocating an award or promotion.

If you criticize "the system," do it in a positive and constructive context. An officer and leader must manifest his faith in the institution that he's a part of. Don't harp on the fact that some aspect of the organization "sucks"; focus on how to make it better and lead the effort to institutionalize an improved procedure or solution. These days, you'll find that senior leaders are highly receptive to innovative changes and improved efficiency, especially when they see that you're enthusiastically trying to improve the organization rather than find fault and point fingers.

The president is your commander in chief and nothing else; if there is any doubt, just take a look at your commissioning certificate. Don't initiate or get drawn into political discussions in which people in uniform are spewing out negative criticism of the incumbent president. If you overhear such banter, you should take measures to terminate it. It might be enough to inject a simple comment such as, "Hey folks, he's doing a really great job as our commander in chief." If that doesn't get the situation in check, then more direct guidance or a direct order from you would be appropriate.

Integrity is everything; any officer who is less than truthful will be crushed by his superiors and ostracized by his peers. If an officer makes a mistake, he simply admits the truth and then stoically endures a few figurative thumps on the head. He will subsequently be forgiven and can then legitimately engage others to help with the discrete fix actions. The same holds true for what gets stated in reports. It's certainly smart to emphasize the positive and downplay the negative. But an officer's integrity and credibility will come into question if the metrics in a report are intentionally distorted or if the unpleasant truth is purposely covered up with thick sugarcoating.

Never whine and complain, not to your subordinates, not to your peers and not to your boss. You are to prevent problems where possible, solve all problems that arise, and achieve the unit goals, even in the face of some very challenging conditions. You can't make all of your people happy all of the time, and you're not going to be happy all the time. When the going gets tough, you have to display a positive attitude and generate optimism. Keep a stiff upper lip, check your bearings, and then enthusiastically charge forward. And remember, it's always harder to fill a half-empty glass than it is to fill one that's already half full.

The old adage "The world is a small place" couldn't be more true than it is in the Air Force. You'll often cross paths with old colleagues throughout your career. Do what you can to ensure that they have favorable memories of their past interactions with you. Furthermore, you'll surely influence the lives of your airmen and be a significant figure in their eyes. Unlike corporate America, many of your people will maintain contact with you long after you've moved on to another assignment, and they'll cheer you on as you move up the promotion ladder.

Chapter 9
BOSS RELATIONS

Although your boss may be a powerful and somewhat intimidating figure; rest assured that senior Air Force officers do not eat their young. The boss might not work hard at getting you to like him, but you may have to work hard at getting him to like you. Reading each other's biography is a starting point for developing a good relationship. And, contrary to the "pin'em where they win'em" philosophy, try and wait until you show up at your new organization to have your award citation read and a medal pinned on your chest. Even if it doesn't happen that way, you and your boss will still eventually get synchronized and share a great deal of mutual respect. Here are a few insights that may help make that happen faster.

  Be totally loyal to your boss and your unit, in every respect and in every situation. This is particularly true when relaying the boss's instructions or orders. If you don't agree with the boss's order, respectfully let him know face to face. If he still wants you to proceed, salute smartly and then "make it happen." Don't weakly echo his order by saying, "We've got to accomplish this senseless task because the boss said so." From his lofty position, your boss has the big picture and can see what's over the horizon; he won't always have enough time to explain it all to you as he gives an order during hectic operations.

Always do everything within your power to make your boss look good, and never let him get caught by surprise. Give him a heads-up on any significant situation, good or bad, before he goes to high level staff meetings or goes out onto the streets. If he's at least alerted that someone may jump out at him with a hot issue or big news, he'll be prepared to deal with it calmly and objectively while amongst his peers or his boss. Even just his confidently spoken words can be enough to reassure the most senior officers. "General, my people are already all over that situation; the permanent fix action they came up with is even going to improve our F-16 sortie generation rates."

When your boss gives an order, he is confident that the people who acknowledge it are going to follow through and deliver results. The words "yes, sir" are absolutely worthless if not followed by the stated or implied action. This also holds true for orders you give. It would be far better to hear an airman say, "I don't think that'll work, L-T" than to hear the hollow words "yes, sir," only to find out later that he didn't fully carry out your order. When an individual questions an order, there's usually some meaningful dialogue to clarify or modify the order. But if the boss simply reiterates the lawful order, it stands and must be carried out.

Enthusiastically agree to do what your boss says needs to be done, but hold back on telling him about how you and your team are going to deliver results way above and beyond what he requested or needs. It's far better to pleasantly surprise the boss with sterling results than it would be to fall short of his expectations, which you may have elevated prematurely and unnecessarily. You can't promise your boss a Porsche Carrera and then deliver a Volkswagen Beetle. But just imagine his reaction when he anticipates getting a Volkswagen and you present him with the Porsche instead.

Don't lure your boss into micromanaging your branch or flight by telling him too much about the ongoing activity. His part of the deal is to provide you with a mission, to ensure you have the resources to do the job, and then stand by for the success story as you and your people get that job done. However, you should occasionally give the boss very brief verbal or e-mail updates so he knows everything is on track. Stay alert to detect and correct problems before he notices; that way he won't be reaching around you, trying to do your job for you. Also, avoid deferring decisions to your boss; you are the officer who controls the activity and destiny of your management domain.

Contemporary leaders don't hire bootlickers. An officer who would try to win the boss's favor via that shameful method won't go far. Actually, that type of behavior is rather obvious and nobody likes it, not even the boss. Furthermore, there is a possibility, albeit very remote, that one of your people might try to get in your good graces using that same method. You'll have to find a subtle but clear way to communicate that strong duty performance is the only way he'll win your respect and admiration. Also, even though someone might accuse you of favoritism, it's OK to favor your strongest performers who deliver topnotch results. Hopefully, your boss will favor you as well.

Don't brag to your boss about how you achieved results. You'll work hard at leading your team to success, and you'll get a feeling of fulfillment from that activity. But when all is said and done, it's about what your people did to achieve the results. View yourself as being just a cut above a spectator when it's time to recognize, praise and reward the folks that actually did the hard and smart work. Your boss will be keenly aware of the role you played as the team leader; in fact, he'll probably give you a quick "thumbs-up" and a smile as he's doling out letters of appreciation and medals to the troops.

Your boss has only so many "silver bullets." When you ask him to fire off a round on your behalf, make sure it's a truly critical issue. Where possible, take care of the issue yourself at your level, perhaps telling your boss about it after the fact. He'll immediately realize that you could have easily and rightfully turned to him for help but didn't, and he'll respect you for having smartly dealt with and resolved a super tough issue at your level. Plus, that silver bullet remains in his bandolier for future use, maybe on an issue that supports or benefits you.

If you need your boss to say something important to the outside world, draft the e-mail for him to launch. He may edit it a bit, or quite a lot, but he'll greatly appreciate your having provided him with a draft. Just put yourself in his shoes and write objectively, using facts rather than emotion. If you know that he has a long-standing rapport with the addressee or it's one of his colleagues at equal staff level, make the tone of the e-mail somewhat more personal and cordial. Let your boss decide himself on courtesy-copy addressees, such as a flag officer or a higher headquarters.

Your boss may sometimes ask you if you're willing to take on a special project; that usually means he has already selected you to handle it and will only reconsider if you pose some reasonable objections. Such tasks are jokingly referred to as "opportunities to excel." Actually, that's just what they are, and the boss might be tasking you just to test your capabilities as a leader and manager. You should cheerfully accept the tasking because, in the end, you'll be demonstrating to him that you're capable of deftly handling most anything, including increased responsibilities. Even though you're the one he tasked, you should bring your NCOs into play where appropriate; that would make it a leadership event.

Be aware that the person who sits directly across from the boss in his staff meeting is likely to walk away from the table with a tasking. Skeptics can test this theory by simply making eye contact with the boss a few times. Also, tasking usually goes to the person who is most likely to deliver success. Carefully and respectfully speak up if all tasks are flowing to you while your colleagues have a relatively light load. If it's common knowledge that your branch is buckling under the load, you'll probably hear a fellow officer chime in to say, "Sir, I've got a real hotshot in that area; if you prefer, my flight could handle that project." Don't forget to return the favor to your colleague when the time is right.

Keep in mind that colonels and chiefs traditionally have a special rapport. Even though a chief has the boss's ear, he's not going to directly critique a young officer's duty performance. However, he might make a cryptic remark such as, "Those guys in the Ops Branch are still trying to get it together, Colonel." You can just imagine what that translates to as your boss or senior rater is pondering your next move in terms of career progression. It's worth noting that warrant officers in the other branches of service technically outrank an Air Force chief, but the Air Force chief is a far more important person than at least the first three warrant officer ranks, and he has similar authority and responsibility

Don't get frustrated with a senior boss who isn't an information technology wizard like you. Even though he wasn't born into the digital generation, the old dinosaur can still learn new tricks. Three factors are in his favor: his tendency to deal with capabilities and processes in terms of systems, the fact that software functionality is becoming more intuitive, and the fact that man-machine interfaces are becoming more user-friendly all the time. Yes, it's imperative that all airmen posses a fair degree of IT savvy, but in the end it's the charismatic and enlightened generalist who will lead the way ahead to victory, not some narrow-minded technocrat.

Senior officers don't need to participate in experiments or beta tests. An overly eager boss might jump to the conclusion that your prototype capability is ready for prime time and then fall on his sword in public. It's like showing your boss a prototype sports car; he's ecstatic about the car, grabs the keys from you, and races down the track. In all the excitement, he didn't hear you explain that the steering hasn't been perfected and the brakes haven't been installed yet. You were his hero until he crashed the car into the guardrail. Of course, if you demo a viable concept, you'll be pressured to quickly bring it to fruition so it can be implemented on a broad scale. That's OK, because your boss will then ensure that you receive all the required resources.

Don't use your BlackBerry or send text messages via the cell phone while your boss is talking to you or chairing a meeting. Your boss will get rather peeved if you start catching up on your e-mail while he's trying to dialogue with you, although your boss might occasionally read and send e-mails in your presence, maybe even while you're speaking to him. When the boss is talking to you, don't even look at your cell phone to see who is calling, the exception being when you and your boss are waiting to get word on a hot, ongoing situation. "Sir, let me see if this call is the update we need."

Do not "shoot from the hip" when answering your boss's e-mails. If you can't provide a good response right away, simply say that you'll jump on the issue immediately and have an answer in short order. Next, get with your people to dig up the facts so you have an understanding of the problem and the root cause of the situation, especially if it's a bad one. Work with your people to devise a course of action. Then let your boss know that you quickly probed the situation and that your team is poised to take the following actions at any time, even right now in the middle of the night if necessary.

Very senior officers cannot read all the long documents they need to sign; therefore, they require a concise explanation of the content of those documents. In some instances this can be done verbally; other times a short note may suffice, or a formal staff summary sheet may even be required. In the "paperless" organization, documents are coordinated and staffed via collaborative tools on the military internet. That's all good, but don't pass the boss a soft copy document that's cluttered with six iterations of editing and coordination. Instead, he should be presented a clean document that's in its final version, ready for signature.

Learn to speak concisely to your boss, and only tell him what he really needs and wants to know. If he needs to know what time it is, he doesn't want an explanation of the inner workings of your Swiss timepiece. And he also doesn't want to hear you anguish over the labor pains as you try to deliver the end product of a big task he assigned to you. Be very careful with the tone of your voice and your body language when communicating with your boss; remain calm, composed and respectful. Your boss will be taking note of your comportment and will admire your ability to remain steady under fire.

There's no escaping the fact that you've got to give your boss both good news and bad news. However, you can often control the timing of the delivery. You don't want to approach the boss when he's so busy or preoccupied that he can't fully absorb the good news, and you don't want to drop bad news on him at a time when he's embroiled in some sort of frustrating battle. In the event you have to give bad news to your boss, devise some positive initiative to help remedy the situation or offer to visit the site of the ongoing problem, as his representative.

Joint assignments are on the rise; you may end up working for an officer of another branch of service. Don't rush to work for Navy officers; most of them don't subscribe to the Air Force culture; they write lukewarm performance reports, and they're stingy with medals. Don't be reluctant to work for Army officers; only the very best of them have survived recurring iterations of force restructuring, and they often treat airmen better than their own soldiers. If you have a Marine boss, stand by for tough but exciting challenges because they always set the bar real high. If you have a Guard or Reserve boss of any branch, he'll probably have a tremendous amount of specialty knowledge based on his civilian profession or business, and a work ethic that's tough to match.

You may eventually have an international officer as your "supervisor." An important part of your job is to help him look good in the eyes of senior U.S. officers on the staff. Also, remember that the foreign officer is your boss in daily activities, but your real boss, wherever he's located, wears a U.S. uniform. Be both respectful of your foreign boss and discretely loyal to your U.S. boss. Don't be too critical of foreign officers who seem a bit distanced from their troops; officers of some countries are considered to be part of the aristocracy. Likewise, don't get flustered over foreign military unions; work around them rather than fight them. Finally, many international officers have hollow legs; don't try to match their pace of alcohol consumption.

It's tough work to craft first-rate promotion recommendations; so give the boss all the help he'll accept on that score. Discretely give him draft phrases, with the requisite sources, for your promotion recommendations. That'll leave him with more time and energy to create a final product. He'll pump up or tone down the volume of your draft text; he'll insert military slang and acronyms, and he'll stratify you amongst your peers. Don't try to argue better stratification for yourself after the fact; you'll just lose your dignity in that futile effort. Your boss and the senior rater have already thought long and hard about where you stand in relation to your peers, which may even be number one.

The first thing to do if you have a monster boss is to conduct a self-assessment to ensure the problem is not you yourself. If your boss really is an overbearing ogre, figure out where you and your boss are compatible; then play up that aspect of your relationship and minimize the out-of-synch areas. Next, learn the triggers that upset the boss and carefully avoid setting those off. Then determine and deliver the type of duty performance that your cranky boss admires. Finally, endeavor to make the best of the situation, with the comforting knowledge that either you or the boss will ultimately be transferred; a legal separation is imminent.

Chapter 10
CAREER PROGRESSION

Although you deserve to be promoted, be aware that careerism per se is an unsavory activity. Promotion is the by-product, not the goal, of an Air Force officer's duties and service, and there's much more substance to an officer's career than mere rank. Nonetheless, you still have to get all the right boxes checked in order to keep your military career on track, even if it's just out of fairness to the officials who are advocating your continued promotion. Obviously, you're always engaged in much more important activity than finagling your own promotions, but there are a few things you should keep in mind.

Mentoring is now institutionalized in the Air Force; however, it's even better if you find one senior person who is willing to coach and encourage you throughout your career. If you can't find a senior officer to informally mentor you on a long-term basis, pick some renowned figure as a role model. Your role model might be a powerful figure like General Curtis "Bombs Away" LeMay, who built up Strategic Air Command, or perhaps General "Chuck" Horner, who ran the air campaign in the first Gulf War. If you happen to opt for a role model from the civilian sector, forget about glitzy people like Ted Turner and Donald Trump.

The Air Force has elite communities, just as in other sectors of society. The prestigious pilots and navigators who wear flight suits, leather jackets and wings are categorized as rated officers, as are the flight surgeons and air battle managers. Fighter pilots are more special than generic aviators who fly transport and refueling aircraft, and even fighter pilots have an elite subset of F-15 pilots (add F-22 and/or F-35 soon). Academy graduates (aka Zoomies or Ring Knockers) are a body of alumni that endures long past graduation. But plain vanilla officers shouldn't be too alarmed about all this. Rated officers, academy grads, and generic nonrated officers are all pretty much on a level playing field as they compete for promotion in the early stages of their careers.

Capitalize on various career broadening opportunities, but don't let your thirst for adventure hurt your boss or colleagues who have to deal with your share of the load while you're gone. Volunteering for a TDY to an exotic location or attending a course that's unrelated to your unit's mission could cause the seniors to perceive you as abandoning them to run off and have fun. You might want to explain the return on investment to your boss. Let him be part of the decision process before you do a secret handshake with a high-level outsider who could use a power play to hire you away, temporarily or permanently. You'll be surprised at how often the altruistic senior officers will support you in such endeavors, as long as they're given a vote.

Career broadening assignments should be within the realm of aviation, or at least be pertinent to the flying community. Not all seniors would see the value in your doing an education-with-industry tour at Microsoft or Sun Microsystems. But it would matter a great deal to everyone if you spent a year working at Lockheed Martin or with Boeing. Actually, few people will really care about your adventure in corporate America unless whatever you're involved in is clearly relevant to aviation and airpower. Remember, Air Force promotion boards are stacked with aviators who are totally focused on airpower.

You can control your own destiny to a certain degree by making yourself the most likely candidate to be chosen for a particular school or assignment. Enroll in a correspondence program to demonstrate your interest in attending the actual school in residence; earn a rating in the foreign language of a country that you want to be assigned to; or become qualified on the flight simulator for an aircraft you hope to transition to. In other words, do what you can to make yourself stand out from the competition. Applying, wishing and hoping are not enough to get selected.

Avoid being assigned to a unit or base that's about to be closed. That's truly a gloom and doom scenario. It's tough for a leader to keep everyone's spirits up as the mission fades away and as unit members scramble to transfer out, without backfills. Plus, you'll constantly be fending off the treasure hunters from nearby bases who try to commandeer equipment and furniture long before your base closes; although, you and your commander may want to judiciously release some premium items to help out another squadron. Even worse, performance reports will lack substance as mission activity starts to diminish. In this case, it may even be smart to loan some of your people to other units where they're needed; at least they'll be gainfully employed and they'll enjoy some self-fulfillment.

Accept the opportunity to become an aide de camp or executive officer if you have great admiration and respect for the senior officer you'll be serving. Be aware that the senior colonel or flag officer who hires you cannot reach into the system to get you promoted as a reward at the end of your tour. He can only help you get the right next assignment, which could lead to promotion if you're successful in it. The other spin-off benefit of working directly for the general is that you'll receive valuable tutoring in officership and leadership, either as a conscious effort on his part or simply because you're always in close proximity to the general.

You'll only be selected to be a squadron commander if you express the desire and demonstrate the requisite qualifications. Start doing that very early on by seeking assignment as a flight commander or detachment commander. Odd as it may seem, there really is no mandate for a career officer to serve as a unit commander. However, not doing so normally sets one's rank ceiling at lieutenant colonel. In this day and age, there's plenty of dignity in retiring at that rank. But the honor of having successfully served as a commander is something you'll carry with you forever.

When you ultimately become a commander, your family will have to understand that command is the most important and demanding assignment of your career. It's best to be up front with them so they understand that for a period of time they'll be number two in your life, even though they're always number one in your heart. They'll be extremely proud of you as a commander, and your spouse will enjoy being a First Lady of sorts. Encourage your spouse to establish a leadership role in some of the squadron-sponsored community activities.

The lady officers should set the time for the proverbial stork to arrive; that is, if their religion offers that latitude. An officer is a "company grader" for about ten years, so there's ample opportunity to plan child-bearing around deployments and prior to or after being a commander. A pregnant lady commander will discover that everyone cheerfully supports her and sincerely wishes her and her family all the happiness in the world. However, there's a likelihood that her boss and some of the senior leaders will wonder why that child-bearing activity, and her associated absence, had to occur during her tenure as a unit commander.

Yes, family does come first in the military, wherever and whenever that happens to be possible. It's important to realize that the quality of the family experience is more important than the quantity of time the family spends together. Bring your family to visit during a squadron open house so they can better understand what your demanding career in the military is all about and where you fit into the big picture. Ensure that your family gets to capitalize on special perks such as formal dining outs, military parades, overseas travel, etc. Foster your family's support for your career progression; they'll cheer you on if they too believe in what you're doing with your life.

Contemplate the future before you embark on matrimony with a foreign national spouse. Satellite TV, the internet, and international commerce have created a global society, but not a single global culture. The foreign spouse's struggle with the English language will seem quaint in the beginning but will later prove to be frustrating in various situations. Also, the transplanted spouse may have such strong ties with family overseas that she feels sort of exiled to live a lonely life on or around an air base. Consider other factors, such as level of your security clearance, validity of her credentials in the U.S., and settings for her to practice a unique religion. Love conquers all; just realize that there might be a few boulders strewn on this blissful path.

There are few bases where you can homestead for very long without appearing to have stagnated in terms of career growth. Like anyone else, military families can enjoy the American dream of home ownership. Nevertheless, you shouldn't cling tightly to a house; doing so diminishes your thirst for bigger and more challenging assignments. It's best for company grade officers to avoid purchasing a home or condo unless it's in a resort area where property values are likely to rise, or it's located where they anticipate ultimately settling down. If you buy a home and then PCS to another location, obtain the services of a professional rental property manager who is a member of a highly reputable national real estate firm. You can't personally deal with rental property problems while you're busy leading your team at a faraway location, oftentimes overseas.

Prepare a complete biography as you pin on the rank of first lieutenant, and keep it as a soft copy for easy updates. In the biography, don't bother stating what high school you graduated from as nobody cares; start the academics section with college. Include relevant professional association memberships such as the National Association of Aeronautical Engineers, but not something like the National Rifle Association or a college fraternity. Awards should be included as well, but they have to be something significant, such as company grade officer of the year at any organizational level, or a professional award at the regional or national level. Include medals but not ones that are almost standard issue, such as the National Defense Medal.

There is some gamesmanship involved in your input to the performance report that the boss will write on you. Packing too many achievements into the first OPR of your assignment may cause the subsequent OPR to look hollow. Some activity that's of a continuing nature could possibly be slipped into the next reporting period. Above all, avoid short reporting periods. In situations where reassignment of your boss would inadvertently trigger an OPR covering a very short reporting period, you have to eliminate the need for that OPR by getting yourself briefly assigned under another officer until the new boss arrives. Don't be shy about asking for this brief change; you'll find that everyone will be pleased you suggested it.

In the event you end up with a government service employee as your boss, his involvement in your career may be little more than asking, "Where do I sign?" That's the question you'll hear as you present a draft performance report or award package. Obviously, you'll have a blue-suit rater somewhere in the chain, but that person may be at a distant location. So, some of your career management activity may have to be conducted in the do-it-yourself mode for a brief period. This isn't a common scenario, but it definitely happens when military officers are filling positions in certain government agencies, which shall remain unnamed.

Check your on-line records on a regular basis, and request a hard copy of your records from the Air Force Personnel Center four months before your promotion board meets. Records are all that the board has as a basis for their promotion decisions. All the blame for flaws or missing items in your records will fall squarely on you alone if you get passed over for promotion, no matter who caused the glitches. Of course, you could protest and try to get promoted via a Supplementary Board, but they rarely overturn previous promotion board results when the protest is based solely on flawed records. Plus, there's only a small chance of getting promoted Above-the-Zone later. If you keep your records current, you'll avoid a "game-over" situation.

Hold back on trying to find out about promotion board results before they are officially published. Your commander is the one who gets the pleasure of surprising you with the good news of your selection for school or promotion. Your troops will also be vicariously enjoying your wonderful news, particularly since they helped make it happen. Consider the chap who kept phoning up the chain of command to find out if he was promoted. Staff personnel at the headquarters stopped his irritating phone calls by simply telling him that he was indeed on the promotion list. He and his family then started celebrating with friends. Unfortunately, his name was not actually on the list when it was posted.

As a fine officer in the early stages of your career, you're surely going to be promoted in what is pretty much a "fully-qualified" selection scenario. But don't get so cocky that you start strategizing for future Below-the-Zone promotion recommendations. Just the fact that an officer resorts to such scheming means that he's probably not one of the chosen few destined for early promotions and a rise to flag officer ranks. Those people seem to stand out as "bigger than life" figures that are on a fast-track to the higher ranks. And once they get on that BTZ train, it just keeps on rolling. If you're not one of them, it's best to stand clear of the tracks and salute the future generals as they go by.

Lady officers successfully rise to the higher ranks in the Air Force; the fabled glass ceiling has been broken and flag officer rank is achievable. But one question still remains: Does the officer get promoted based on her charm and the need to meet a human relations quota, or does she get promoted based on duty performance and cumulative achievements? Fortunately, things have evolved to the point where her promotion is indeed based on merit, and a lady officer does not need to be "more equal" than her male counterparts. Nevertheless, female officers should still seize on any opportunity to discuss career progression with a lady colonel or a general, if for no other reason than to gain further reassurance and encouragement.

Some officers might find hard work, long duty hours, and extensive travel to be arduous. Except for occasional stints in a combat zone, a civilian executive can expect much the same, but his high-stress mission is largely pursuit of the almighty dollar. As an Air Force officer, you're engaged in more noble and exciting endeavors; plus, family and friends hold you in much higher esteem than an aggressive stockbroker, a slick marketer, or an ambulance-chasing law school grad. When the military road seems steep and bumpy, remember that what you find to be problematic in the Air Force may simply be one of life's universal challenges. If you exit into the corporate world, you'll rediscover the same problem and still have to deal with it.

No matter how exasperated or frustrated you might feel at the end of a particularly tough duty day, do not utter the words, "I'm getting out." People will take your words to heart, even if only at a subconscious level. Then you might be marked as someone who is leavening the team, or even abandoning it. Although making such a declaration is not supposed to affect your ongoing career, doing so prematurely could inadvertently impact you in many ways: assignment selection, school nomination, and promotion recommendation. In other words, you might unintentionally seal your fate now and deeply regret it later.

Sure you're proud to serve your country, but for your own financial security, you might be thinking, "Show me the money!" Well, you've got a good paying position as an Air Force officer, but that alone won't make you rich. Therefore, be somewhat frugal, and only make low-risk, long-term investments so that you'll have complete peace of mind as you carry on with your duties. Some financial managers and institutions are more honorable than others; keep your shield up to defend against the aggressive vultures. Your real compensation is the prestige of being an Air Force officer, the camaraderie you share with fellow airmen, and the opportunity to be a leader on a stage that's way bigger than any in hometown USA. Yes, you'll eventually achieve financial comfort, but in the final analysis you're all about "Service before self."

Obviously, you're an exceptionally fine Air Force officer on your own merits. But don't discount luck as an element of your success. Even though you might occasionally make a slightly flawed decision, Lady Luck will sometimes intervene to make everything come out just right. Oftentimes, your good luck is simply a matter of being in the right place at just the right time.

Conversely, keep at least a notional plan B in mind so you can keep everything on track in the event that you encounter a bit of bad luck. In any case, stay postured to quickly capitalize on good luck when it comes your way. If that's a short-notice assignment to a new base or school, be ready to be shot out of the cannon to reach even greater heights in your Air Force career.

Chapter 11
PARTING THOUGHTS

If General "Hap" Arnold could talk to us from the heavens above, he'd probably say, "Wow, you guys have taken my Air Force way beyond B-17 Flying Fortresses and P-51 Mustangs." The Air Force the general created now operates in the air, in outer space and in cyberspace. The general would be perplexed by stealth aircraft, airborne lasers, and micro aerial vehicles. He'd be further stymied by cyber warfare, network-centric operations, and airmen training in the virtual battlespace. But in the end, the general would declare, "Technological advances may facilitate all this transformation, but my airmen remain as the one constant of superior airpower."

As an Air Force officer leading fellow airmen, you'll have to stay physically tempered and mentally agile. You'll need to maintain full situational awareness and be postured to embrace changes that enhance mission capabilities, using fewer resources. If you're an effective leader, your airmen will enthusiastically abandon obsolete systems and practices while incorporating new technology and methods. And they'll find all of that important activity to be intrinsically rewarding. In the end, you'll be amazed to discover that they'll exceed your expectations, and because of you they'll even excel beyond their own expectations—they'll grow!

Make sure that your presence as an officer inspires your subordinates and impresses your seniors. As you surge forward in your career, listen to the voice of experience, and listen to that little voice in the back of your head when you feel that you may be pushing the envelope a bit too far. Try to achieve some balance in your life; work hard and play hard, doing both safely. Pull your family into your military life so that they can appreciate your calling and support you, whether you're at home station or deployed overseas. Rest assured that if you perform well as a company grade officer, your commanders will get you promoted all the way up to the rank of major.

During your time in the Air Force, you'll have exciting moments when the adrenalin is pumping through your veins extremely fast. Some officers will consider that to be excessive stress and opt out of the game; other officers will thrive on it and become adrenalin junkies as they enjoy success on a fast-moving playing field. Whether you serve in the Air Force for just four years or for thirty years, it's important that you walk away from the experience with your head held high, knowing you always did your very best and served your country with great honor. You'll ultimately look back on these years as the ones in which you truly lived life to the fullest, as a commissioned officer in the world's greatest Air Force!

ABOUT THE AUTHOR

Colonel John C. Liburdi was born and raised in Milwaukee, Wisconsin. He obtained his bachelors degree in psychology from the University of Maryland, and he earned his masters degree in management from Troy State University. He attended the full range of Air Force officer professional development schools in-residence, including Senior Service School, and he earned various technical and engineering credentials. He served in the Navy for six years, and he spent the remainder of his forty year active duty career in the Air Force. Twenty-nine years of his military service were spent overseas in foreign countries. The Colonel held thirteen different military ranks, including Master Sergeant. He was also a Joint Service Officer.

Colonel Liburdi worked primarily in the Telecommunications Systems and Information Technology career fields, managing both operations and maintenance. He served a tour as Chief of the Technical Services Division in a Joint Chiefs of Staff sponsored organization that provides specialized support to overseas military operations. He served as the Deputy Director of a Joint Test and Evaluation program focused on Battle Damage Assessment. He also served a tour as the U.S. Chief of Security Assistance in the country of Italy to support their F-16, AV-8 and C-130 aircraft programs, including aircraft armaments and defense systems. He commanded a communications squadron for three years; his unit won two Air Force Outstanding Unit Awards. In his last assignment, he served as Chief of the Network Systems Division for the U.S. Air Force in Europe, overseeing the management and modernization of communications, computer, meteorological, navigation and landing systems.

Colonel Liburdi received numerous awards and decorations, including the Armed Forces Expeditionary Medal, seven Meritorious Service Medals, the Air Force Legion of Merit Medal, and the Defense Superior Service Medal. The Colonel retired in 2007 and now resides near Charlotte, North Carolina.